In Kerry, in the olden days, cows were kept indoor on May Day—otherwise bad-minded people might steal a little of their milk and 'enchant' them, so that they would produce nothing but foam for the year.

Superstitious belief was deeply entrenched. Fairies, who lived in the old ring-forts, were constantly trying to lure humans away with their enchanted music, or steal unguarded children. Anyone foolish enough to go walking at night might encounter Jackie-the-Lantern with his ghostly trail of light, the black dog of Callinafercy, the pooka, or—most dreaded of all—the headless coachman. A wealth of omen abounded, to predict the weather, warn of impending ill-luck or death, and ordain the right day to start fishing (Friday, if possible) or school (never on Friday). Prosperity could be ensured by keeping sixpence under a statue of the Infant Jesus of Prague, and if age-old cures for illness didn't work, for any reason, there was always the holy well, which was never known to fail.

Life could be hard. The *spailpín fanách* still wandered the roads in the thirties, while underlying the gaiety of the 'American wake' was the sad reality that the emigrant would probably never see home or country again. But there was also fun and laughter, and evenings at 'rambling houses', with *sean nós* singing, music on the violin, melodeon and *bodhran*.

I Heard the Wild Birds Sing captures the richness of the folk culture of Kerry—in custom, belief, superstition, religious practice, local history—bringing alive in a gently humorous way, life on land and river, the festivals of the year, school and holidays, the local big house.

PATRICK O'SULLIVAN

I Heard the Wild Birds Sing

A KERRY CHILDHOOD

Illustrated by

AL O'DONNELL

ANVIL BOOKS

For my father and mother,
Patrick and Ellen O'Sullivan

First published in 1991 by
Anvil Books
45 Palmerston Road, Dublin 6

© Text Patrick V. O'Sullivan
© Illustrations Anvil Books

ISBN 0 947962 55 7

Typesetting by Computertype Ltd.
Printed by Colour Books, Dublin.
Cover photograph: Bord Failte

Contents

Introduction

My mother's favourite poet was Francis Ledwidge and the poem of his that I remember most vividly is the lament for Thomas MacDonagh. At the time (though I was later to meet the *bonnán buí* at school) the bittern meant nothing to me, and my childhood recollection of the first line was: *He shall not hear the wild birds sing.*

How sad that seemed to me! growing up in countryside where the seasons of the year were chronicled by the songs of birds, from the raucous cawing of the rooks in March, to the sad, thin, winter song of the robin at year's end. Summer began with the coming of the swallows, the sound of the cuckoo echoing from distant glens, and the corncrakes calling to each other from the hay meadow in the long hot nights. Goldfinches twittered in waste places, and blackbirds, thrushes, chaffinches and willow warblers ushered in each dawn with full-throated ease. One of my earliest memories is of my mother taking me in her arms and lifting me high to peer at a nest of open-mouthed *gearrcachs* or young blackbirds in their nest, hidden in a tangle of budding branches.

Nature was part of the very fabric of life. Spring was primroses and daffodils and gorse. The hawthorn trees were snowy drifts of blossom in May, the heavy scent of honeysuckle filled the air on sultry June days and, from August on, the hills were soft with the purple of ling and heather. Even the sea-shore bloomed with pale and delicate colour—pretty sea pinks, wild campion and the salt-loving sea-aster with its daisy-like flowers. We caught occasional glimpses of handsome red foxes in the woods, even heard the shuffle of foraging badgers at dusk, and watched the hares leaping and sparring with each other on spring evenings.

My mother and father were gentle people who took great pleasure in the simple things of life. My mother loved country walks and flowers and her hens. My father's interests were boats and fishing. They took great pride in their work, whether it was a warm cake of bread on the table (its wonderful nutty aroma filling the kitchen) or a finely crafted rick of turf in the yard. They were deeply but quietly religious and yet they always seemed to be tolerant of other people's views and beliefs.

There is no heritage more vibrant and colourful than living folk culture, the *béaloideas* of a people, and in this book I have tried to capture the richness of the Kerry tradition— in custom, belief, superstition, religious practice, local history. It is a story about seemingly ordinary people and their everyday lives, a record of what Listowel writer Bryan MacMahon has described as 'the minor epiphanies of the passing day'.

The material has come from personal recollections and conversations with members of the older generation in Callinafercy and Milltown. I would like to thank the Head of the Folklore Department at University College, Dublin, for permission to publish some extracts from the folklore archives. Other sources include Victorian travel books and periodicals.

And just as my interest in things past was kindled by the old storytellers around the hearth on long winter nights, talking in soft voices while the flames danced and crackled, perhaps this tribute to a marvellously colourful way of life, that in the space of just thirty years has become little more than a memory, will light a spark for a generation to whom it is already a lost world.

Patrick V. O'Sullivan

1
Home and Family

When I was growing up in the fifties, we lived in a yellow-washed cottage fronted by a long narrow flower garden and an irregular privet hedge. It had been built in the mid-thirties on a hill not far from the nearby River Laune, a splendid location that looked towards the broad expanse of Dingle Bay, and was partially constructed with stones from an eighteenth-century wall that surrounded the tiny cottage where my father had been born. Because of its lofty situation, the older people who were never, in the Kerry tradition, at a loss for a name or a nickname, christened it 'the Lighthouse'. On the advice of Major Marshall, owner of Callinafercy, our local big house, the gable faced north towards the road, so that the front door would not have to withstand the fury of the strong northerly gales that swept in from the bay.

The garden was dominated by the large sycamore-tree which had been planted by my mother. In springtime there were primroses, winking with dew, and daffodils blossomed profusely everywhere. My mother took special delight in planting them in clusters along the ditches of the tiny field beyond the front garden, and so, as our little brown donkey grazed contentedly in the field, he seemed marooned in a sea of yellow as they swayed and waved all around him. Beyond the hedge, inside the whitewashed wall beside the road, was a forsythia bush which my mother had grown from a cutting taken from the garden of Callinafercy. This was a mass of yellow blossoms in spring while almost directly across the road a lone furze was an even more dazzling splash of yellow-gold. But the most vivid of all the spring flowers were the wine-red wallflowers that filled the air with their soft perfume.

In summer, the daffodils and wallflowers were superseded by dahlias and hollyhocks, carnations, lilies and pink moss-roses, while old country roses, rich and red and sweetly scented, grew up through the hedge at irregular intervals. Planted at the base of the front wall of the cottage was a row of ornamental shamrocks, their pink and white blossoms interspersed with stones and brash red geraniums in brightly painted tins—we never had flower-pots, only old tins and cans which we painted and which proved to be quite attractive. I loved this flowering scented garden, though to an expert there would have seemed to be no order or formality in it at all.

I also had my own little garden, and Mrs. Ruth, Major Marshall's daughter, encouraged my interest in flowers. On one occasion she brought me a present of ornamental daisies which she called 'bachelor's-buttons', and these I treated with a special kind of reverence and care.

Flowers had a very special place in my mother's life. She said spring had not finally come until one could cover a cluster of daisies with one's shoe. Likewise, summer had not arrived until the cuckoo flower, with its raceme of pale violet flowers, blossomed in damp places. She knew every flower that grew around us. The honeysuckle was known locally as the woodbine, and she loved placing its fragrant blossoms—yellowish-white and sometimes tinged with orange—in a jar on the kitchen window ledge. Another familiar flower on banks and in ditches in Callinafercy was the foxglove, its thimble-shaped purple blooms growing on tall slender stems; the tubular flowers, which opened from the bottom of the stem upwards, were known to us as 'fairy fingers'. Less attractive were the clinging cleavers or goosegrass which sometimes stuck to our clothes. The fragile bell-shaped blooms of the greater bindweed, soft and white with a hint of pink, festooned the hedgerows. Here also grew the scrambling tufted vetch with its purplish pea-like blooms, while sometimes in damp places we came across the meadow cranesbill with its brilliant blue flowers.

At the back of our cottage was a small yard with three great palm-trees, which could be seen from a great distance because of their elevated position, planted in a row. One of them subsequently collapsed against the roof of the cottage during a violent storm in the early sixties. My mother's love of flowers was again very much in evidence. There were clumps of pink hydrangeas, a traditional yellow tea-rose, Michaelmas daisies and a chestnut-tree which had been grown from seed. She was always planting seeds, especially apple seeds, a few of which grew into large drooping crab-trees laden with blossoms as perfect and as beautiful as any cherry-tree in springtime. The apples were edible but could not be preserved, no matter how we tried.

Turkeys, hens, geese and ducks roamed the yard, and we had four small limewashed sheds, one for our little donkey in wintertime, another for Rover, the brown and white sheepdog, during the night, a third for farm tools and implements, and a fourth which served as an attic. There was an attic in the house, above the kitchen, but because the ceiling was so high we never used it. Smaller sheds made of iron sheets housed the hens and turkeys.

The cottage consisted of a kitchen which doubled as a living-room, a back kitchen and three bedrooms. My brother and I shared one of the smaller bedrooms, my sister and grandmother another, while our parents slept in the third, larger bedroom.

The two smaller bedrooms were separated, not by a wall but by a partition of white boards. The high cathedral ceiling was formed of long narrow boards, painted with a kind of white paste which very often flaked when dry and fell upon us in bed. I can still remember those white flakes tumbling down from time to time, sometimes falling unseen when we were asleep.

A great black iron bed, a wardrobe and a chair represented the furniture of one of the bedrooms. A trunk which had been brought from America by a visiting aunt, sometime in the thirties, served as a chest for storing clothes in one room while a painted tea-chest performed a similar function in another. There was linoleum on the floors, sometimes purchased in local shops, sometimes from travelling hawkers who called at the door on a regular basis in those days. It was the early sixties before we managed to find the money to buy our first dressing-table, complete with drawers, and didn't we feel grand! Of course there were holy pictures on all the walls and over my bed was a picture of Christ surmounted by the letters INRI.

One of my earliest recollections is of my mother trying to coax and cajole me into falling asleep in the big old iron bed. She had great patience—in total contrast to my father who had none—but sometimes even her considerable reserves were drained and she would tell me that if I didn't fall asleep in a hurry I would be sure to see the big black dog that regularly roamed the countryside near our cottage. My sleeping moments were sometimes filled with awesome visions of that great black dog, whose sole purpose in life was to exact retribution from 'stubborn headstrong little boys who would not fall asleep for their mother'. I didn't know at the time that that very same story of the fiercesome black dog had been told to generation after generation of Callinafercy children; since the late 1800s, and possibly long before, the story of the *madra ciar dubh* had been a popular favourite with mothers at bedtime.

Another vivid memory that stays with me is of the stormy nights when our little cottage, high on the hill, was lashed and battered by howling winds. And yet we children were rarely afraid. My mother told us that she liked being in bed on stormy nights; somehow it gave her a sense of warmth and security and she passed that feeling on to us.

The kitchen, in contrast to my small bedroom, was vast and spacious and it, too, had a high cathedral ceiling, formed of boards that were autumn brown in colour. Whenever my father wanted to paint it, at least three tables of varying size had to be stacked one on top of the other, with a chair perched high on the summit. Holy pictures hung on the rough-cast walls of gleaming white—we seemed to be forever whitewashing the walls with buckets of milk-white lime.

Behind one holy picture was a piece of holly, specially preserved from the preceding Christmas; behind another was a sprig of 'the blessed palm', collected on Palm Sunday. Below the picture of the Sacred Heart was a sacred-heart lamp, from which was suspended a smaller picture of the Virgin Mary. On a press near one of the side walls was a statue of Our Lady, a vase of flowers, some trays, including a Guinness tray with a brightly billed toucan, an ornamental horseshoe and a glazed pottery plate bearing the images of John Fitzgerald and his wife Jacqueline, who seemed to have been imbued with a kind of sainthood in rural Ireland in the late fifties and early sixties.

Electricity did not come to Callinafercy until September 1956 and we had no stove until the mid-sixties. The great hearth or open fireplace was thus the focus of activity in the house for most of my childhood, and it was the only way of cooking for my mother and the women of her generation. The area round it was limewashed from time to time, the whiteness of the lime contrasting with the blackness of the soot which, during damp rainy weather, soiled and stained the whitewashed part with depressing regularity.

Our hearth was of massive proportions and our cat, a large white creature with black markings, was continually snuggled before it, much to the displeasure of my uncle who said that cats should be kept outdoors. The hearth, however, did not contain the large wooden seat ranged on one side of the fire, which was commonplace in many rural households of the fifties. Neither did it have a 'cubby hole' in the brickwork for storing pipes and tobacco. Many hearths in the locality were surmounted by a large shelf, sometimes called a clevvy, on which were displayed tins and boxes of various shapes and sizes. Particularly decorative were the colourful tea-tins, often received as presents from benevolent aunts and uncles.

The iron crane—an upright iron pivot with a projecting

arm—had been made by a local blacksmith. It was well stocked with hangers and hooks of every kind, all of which were used for hanging a plethora of pots and other cooking utensils. Some of the hangers were simply made; others were quite sophisticated, with holes and stoppers to adjust the height of the kettle or pot over the fire. The old-fashioned black kettle, which was exceptionally heavy, even when empty, was treated as something of an heirloom because it had been in the family for decades.

It was on the open fire that my mother made her soda bread in the pot oven. The ingredients were flour and sour milk, leavened with bi-carbonate of soda. When the texture of the dough was smooth, it was flattened, shaped, and cut with the sign of the cross; no cake would bake well without the sign of the cross, my mother said. The dough was placed in the oven which was covered and hung over the fire, then glowing coals were placed on top of the cover to achieve an even temperature. My mother sometimes made chunky apple pies in this way too, and the heat of the fire glowed on her face as she leaned over from time to time, in her blue and white bib, to add more coals to the cover at regular intervals. A neighbour made what she called 'griddle bread'. The dough was worked into a flat thin circular shape which was baked on a thin iron plate over the fire. This plate or griddle was about sixteen inches in diameter and the cake was turned half-way through the cooking time. The dough was again marked with the sign of cross before baking.

My mother often told us that the flour-bags in the old days were printed with an impression of the face of Daniel O'Connell. When the stock of flour was running low, old people in her native place would observe disconsolately, 'Daniel O'Connell, your head is going down.' Such flour-bags, when empty, were washed and used in the making of sheets and pillow-cases.

My earliest and perhaps most vivid recollection of the

household hearth is of those times when my mother allowed me to chop up a leaf of cabbage and boil it in water in a small tin cup placed on top of the glowing coals. The splutter and bubble of the cabbage in the water is one of the distinctive sounds of childhood that will always stay with me. Another memory is of my uncle Donal inserting a poker into the fire, which he then plunged into a mug of porter. The glossy black liquid instantly produced a frothy head, winking with beaded bubbles. This was known as 'mulling' the porter and some houses had a special mulling tongs or poker.

Over the fireplace was a black and white picture of a group of workmen saying the angelus in a newly ploughed field near the sea. My grandmother had seen the picture in a newspaper and had ordered a copy. Not far away was a large tilly lamp or oil lamp, an essential item in the days before electricity. Probably the only modern item of equipment we possessed was the black and cream Mullard radio which stood on a shelf.

The brown dresser had a lower press, with three rows of open shelving above it. Pride of place on the top shelf went to the gleaming lustre jugs which came in a great variety of styles and sizes. These jugs were quite expensive and not everyone could afford them. My grandmother from Claodach—my mother's mother—was something of an expert in cutting potatoes, and once, when she had meticulously prepared the seed for sowing, a grateful neighbour gave her one of the lustre jugs which she admired so much. Jam was sold in jugs in country shops during the twenties and thirties and a few of them were also displayed on the upper shelf. The decoration was rich and varied—charming rustic scenes, handsome dark-blue willow designs, flowers and fruit motifs, fairytale cameos such as Red Riding Hood complete with her well-stocked basket of groceries, and wild forest flowers. The very popular Victorian motif of the fern appeared again and again.

The second shelf held cups, saucers and plates, and the bottom one platters, mugs and bowls. We had dark blue and bright blue meat platters but my aunt had a magnificent glazed brown and cream one, which had an exotic castle design with highly stylised oriental figures in the foreground. Bowls were much in use as drinking vessels during the thirties and forties, but by the fifties their function was generally limited to storing milk or eggs.

The windows of the kitchen had fine lace half-curtains, the material for which could be purchased inexpensively in local shops. The massive table was covered with oilcloth. There was a huge cupboard for storing clothes beside the fire and one of our most innovative childhood games involved pitching all the neatly folded clothes on to the floor, clambering inside and playing 'motor car'. There were very few cars in the area at that time—we travelled everywhere on foot or on a bicycle or by donkey and cart— so we were fascinated by this new miracle of science. My brother was always the driver since he was in possession of the wheel, an old enamel plate, while my sister and I were eternally demoted to the role of back-seat passengers. My mother went about sighing and saying she would be mortified if anyone came in and saw the clothes scattered all over the floor. Indeed she must have had many such moments of despair because in winter and bad weather the kitchen was our play area. We played house, which consisted of two chairs, placed some distance apart, the backs of the chairs facing each other and draped with my grandmother's shawl. Card–games were the perennial favourites, with marbles (when I went to school) coming a close second. We drew a circle of chalk on the old cement floor, placed four marbles inside the circle and attempted to knock them out of the circle by rolling others along the floor. Sometimes the marbles went whizzing under the dresser and we lay flat on our stomachs trying to locate them with the tongs. My father's patience really gave out when we played blindman's-buff; he said we were always making *clampar* and 'the house was like a bawdy-house'.

The small back kitchen was really a porch in which stood the family bin, a wooden chest with a sloping lid. It was divided into two compartments, one of which held white flour, the other yellow meal. The meal which had been eaten by the family in previous decades was reserved, in the fifties, for the hens. Also in the porch was a wash-stand and pan, a larger tin pan for washing clothes, a tin bath for bathing members of the family, a press for holding saucepans and other cooking utensils and a tea-chest which was filled with turf from the rick in the yard.

Mention of baths reminds me of the trauma of hair washing! When we children were reluctant to have our hair washed, my mother told us that if we didn't, one of the herons that made their home in the nearby grove would swoop down and carry us off—so that we might be seen by all and sundry dangling at the end of its long legs. Herons had always been known to have a liking for children with unwashed hair, she insisted. I usually gave up the struggle, but my sister sometimes sought refuge in the ducks' house to escape both hair washing and herons. The heron was a familiar sight on the strand at the Cliff and was known locally as the 'Sheila roggy' or 'the Judy-the-banks'.

In common with all the households around about, our house had no piped water until the early sixties and so my mother and I walked every day to a well which was located in a field about half a mile away. One of the loveliest times of the year for those walks was the month of May, when the ditch near our house was covered with primroses, fragile splashes of yellow and white. On our way back from the well we always picked some which were placed in a jar before the statue of the Virgin in the kitchen window. Wild bluebells were collected too and branches of the sycamore tree, which grew in the garden and which we called the

'summer tree', and they were brought into the house on May Day. That practice of collecting flowers in maytime made such an impression on me that I later wrote the following little verse:

> We knew of love and laughter,
> The joy of simple things.
> We heard the vibrant music
> That the green earth sings.
> We brought in spreading branches,
> Rays from the summer tree.
> Pale primroses we gathered too,
> And cowslips wild and free.
> Blue was the Virgin's mantle,
> Blue as the woodland bells.
> And these were the flowers I gave to her,
> Picked in the sheltered dells.

If the walk to the well represented the romantic aspect of our lives in those days, the lack of piped water added to the daily drudgery. Washing anything was quite an undertaking. When my mother wanted to wash the rough cement floor, she first of all had to boil the water in a big pot. When it was boiled the pivoting crane was swung away from the flames and the water drained into another vessel. My mother knelt on the floor and using a scrubbing brush and common soap (as distinct from toilet soap) washed the floor section by section. It then received at least two rinsings with clean water. And woe betide anyone who put foot in the kitchen until the floor was dry!

Clothes were boiled in a big black pot, and sometimes when the cover had been mislaid, huge lumps of soot fell into the boiling clothes and my mother would have to start her work all over again. Those clothes which could not be boiled were washed in a large tin pan or in a wooden tub. A few of our neighbours had scrubbing boards but my mother did not. When the clothes were ready to iron, heavy hand-irons, large and small, were placed near the blazing fire, and the bases wiped clean before coming into contact with the clothes. A more up-to-date implement was the box iron. This had a hollow compartment into which was placed a heavy piece of iron, similarly shaped, which had been heated until red-hot in the fire. The base of the iron always remained smooth and shining so the constant cleaning was unnecessary. It was not until 1959 that an electric iron made its appearance in the house.

Food was wholesome if simple. Soda bread was baked every day and we ate it with butter—margarine was not popular. We owned a single Kerry cow which supplied all the milk we needed. Great pots of potatoes were boiled for our dinner and pots of smaller potatoes were cooked for the farmyard fowl and animals. This was very much my mother's work and she was forever running to and fro with big pots and small pots and crooked black hangers. Bacon in various forms was the usual choice of meat, often stored by suspending it from hooks in the rafters. When a pig was killed, the meat was salted in a wooden barrel for a period of two weeks, and families had crubeens or pigs' feet—which were boiled with cabbage—and a supply of tasty black puddings, which were carefully made and stored according to time-honoured tradition.

My young world was dominated by family—my mother, my father and my paternal grandmother, who was known locally as 'old Cait'. She was usually dressed in a blouse and dark cardigan over a long black skirt which concealed her red flannel petticoat. She wore a dark three-cornered shawl with a fringe of tassels whenever she went for a stroll or visited the neighbours' houses. She regularly took me with her on these short walks.

She often told us stories of the time she was rearing her large family in the tiny cottage on the edge of the River Laune, in the early decades of the century. Meals consisted of 'spuds and sladdie', sladdie being the old people's name for a curious kind of white sauce. Potatoes, she told us, were then eaten in even greater quantities than in the fifties. The contents of the pot were turned straight on to the scrubbed wooden table, so that clouds of smoke rose in swirls to the rafters above. When one of my uncles emigrated to America some years later, he reminisced, 'God be with the days when we couldn't see each other with the steam from the spuds.' The family at that time had no land of their own, so the potatoes had to be grown on land rented from a nearby farmer, under the conacre system. As they had no money they had to pay their rental 'by the sweat of their brow'. When neighbours called they might see mackerel, or much more rarely pieces of bacon, hanging from the rafters; when the latter was observed, one of the old men would surely say, 'John D.(my grandfather) is after killin' a pig. We'll have atin' and drinkin' for weeks.'

Bread was a staple item of diet. Yellow meal bread, made from a mixture of yellow meal and flour, was a favourite in the twenties. A variation, 'mixed' bread, was made from meal and flour mixed in equal proportions to produce a subtle difference in taste each time. Yellow squares were made simply from yellow meal to which boiling water had been added; the resulting paste was divided into squares and baked. Oatmeal was sometimes steeped in sour milk until it stiffened into a paste which was then baked, and there were various forms of potato bread. The original potato cake consisted of potatoes, boiled and mashed with salt and butter; they were then mixed with flour, flattened and baked on a griddle. Stampy or boxty was often considered a seasonal treat for November nights; raw potatoes were grated and mixed with salt and flour before being baked on a griddle. Wheat, boiled in water for most of the day until it became soft and smooth, was known as *granscahan*: it was then eaten with sugar and new milk. Another form of boiled wheat was known as flummery.

My grandmother washed her clothes in an old tin bath with water from the river, always watching for the low-water tide because she believed that then there would be less salt in the river. The men would be unloading the fish from the boat on the strand and sometimes one or two neighbours would run to help them. They would splash in the water, their trousers upturned, revealing the coarse flannel drawers which they wore underneath. The fish had then to be taken by donkey and cart to Killorglin and that was part of my grandmother's daily routine, from the opening of the fishing season on 17 January every year until it closed on 1 August.

The River Maine was also the source of the primitive lights of those days. An old woman from Milltown described to me how, as a young girl in the early 1900s, she would go down to the bank of the river every evening after school hours to cut rushes which were later peeled and left to dry. The slender cores were then drawn through melted tallow in a grisset, and when the tallow had hardened about it each rush provided ten to fifteen minutes of light. Failing that, if there was a piece of bog deal on the fire, a splinter could be broken from it and placed in a tin on the table.

My grandmother drank the very occasional bottle of porter, 'for the good of her health', but one of her greatest delights was to savour a fresh cup of tea. When her friend Ellie Mary came to visit she often brought with her a gift of a pound of tea, which my grandmother received with as much delight as if it were a pound of gold. As a child I was often amazed at this, unaware that tea had been a scarce and very expensive commodity for poor households during most of her lifetime. The tea was treated with the respect that a connoisseur might accord to a rare and precious wine, and she would usually drink it from one of her fine china cups, which were wafer thin and decorated with curious oriental designs. She had another weakness; it really irked her to find herself without a ready supply of snuff.

My sister seemed to delight in plaguing my grandmother and yet there was a special bond of love between them. On one occasion my sister wanted to play 'dolls and prams' very badly, but since she had neither doll nor pram the situation seemed hopeless. However, having determined that the old rusty wheelbarrow would make a pram of sorts, she badgered and pestered my grandmother into playing the part of the doll. The poor woman reluctantly clambered into the wheelbarrow, her old black skirt draped in ruffles around her. At first the game proceeded uneventfully, my sister making a model mother, but before long my grandmother found herself lying in a clump of nettles, the wheelbarrow overturned beside her. There was a long and heated quarrel afterwards. My sister insisted that it had been a terrible accident. My grandmother and I wondered if that was the whole truth. My sister hated school, especially the sewing and knitting classes, and often swore all sorts of deadly vengeance on the teacher.

My father loved the river and the sea. The salt water was in his blood, he said. He was a perfectionist, which meant that he spent a great deal of time mending nets and repairing boats before the fishing season began. In general, however, patience was not one of his virtures. My mother and I usually cycled to first mass in Killorglin and if ever we happened to be delayed my father would grimly inform us that 'he'd have been on his knees to Cromane' in the

same time. The sting of the jibe lay in the distances—
Killorglin was only three miles away while Cromane was
eight.

If any job seemed to him to be taking an inordinate length
of time he would declare that it was 'going on longer than
Cahir Chapel'; the church at Cahirciveen had taken much
longer to complete than anticipated and the saga of its
construction was part of local folklore. Occasionally when
some utensil or tool went missing he would impatiently
say, 'I put it there a minute ago and the hands of man
must have taken it.' One morning, when I was very small,
he went about the house searching for his shaving-brush,
his chin lathered with soap and wrinkles of indignation on
his forehead; my mother said she just 'hadn't the heart to
tell him he was holding it in his hand'. When my sister
grew into her teens and stayed out late at a dance he would
pace around the massive cold stone floor of the kitchen
calling down vengeance on all and sundry, particularly on
her, but when she returned, all was instantly forgiven, and
all was harmony and light again.

Though I scarcely realised it at the time, my father worked
long and hard. During the winter he worked as a labourer
on the roads, sometimes in places far from home, which
meant rising very early to cycle through wind and rain to
the work site for the day. He went in the darkness of the
morning and came home in the darkness of the evening.
When winter gales damaged the river banks he worked with
other locals to repair the damage. A well-stacked rick of
turf or a well constructed cock of hay gave him the greatest
pleasure. They did not represent just jobs of work. They
were artistic creations; things of beauty to be appreciated
and admired. He believed firmly in the efficacy of holy
water. When a few rows of potatoes had been planted, they
were sprinkled with holy water. When the fishing season
began, a tiny bottle of holy water was placed on the bottom
of the boat, while a holy candle was embedded in one of

the corks or floats on the net.

My father and mother quarrelled very rarely, but they did sometimes have a minor disagreement. If my mother spent too long on a visit to town, he would be sure to say on her return, ' 'Tis the grandeur that's killing ye.' My mother's 'grandeur' consisted of a good green coat, an old black bicycle and a message-bag made from squares of different colours. They were very much in love; we could perceive that clearly though they rarely expressed their emotions in any public kind of way.

The most vivid and enduring memory of my childhood in the small but warm-hearted cottage is of my mother, in her blue print bib, telling stories beside the fire. Very often we were joined by our friends and we sat on cushions on the cement floor, ranged round a frying-pan of potatoes that had just been cooked on the open fire. Some of the stories were variations of universal folk-tales, suitably embellished with local additions and allusions. Other stories seemed to be as home-spun as the yarn she used for darning our socks and jumpers, and indeed she often told her stories while she darned my father's big grey woollen working socks. We hung on every word she uttered and she instilled in us all a love of stories and story-telling.

My mother was religious, not in a dogmatic way but with a simple faith that saw no distinction between living and religious belief. In moments of the greatest crisis, there was always hope and confidence in the mercy of God, expressed in such phrases as 'God is good' or 'We'll have to trust in God'. Heaven was to her as real as earth, and one of her prayers was that 'we may all be happy in our heavenly home one day'.

My childhood memories are not only of people. The countryside around our cottage was, to us, the world. Visitors who came to our house often remarked, 'Ereh, aren't ye spoilt by the grand views,' and indeed we were. For not only was the splendour of Dingle Bay ever-present and enduring; the sun rose every morning above the majestic McGillycuddy and sank in a blinding reddish-haze behind dark Sliabh Mish. Late on summer evenings languid strands of sunlight rippled across the tide and the trees about the old ringed fort on the cliff-top above the bay became just dark silhouettes against the warm red glow of the sinking sun. The fort and the cliff, the trees and the black Kerry cattle, the bay, the mountains and the deep red fire of the sun all combined to create an world of unforgettable beauty. We often went to the strand, sat on a 'port' and bathed our legs in the evening tide, while the waves tumbled gently and soothingly towards the shore. Swans—serene graceful creatures—sheltered near the river banks in winter-time. Great flocks of lapwing, which we called *pilibins*, collected in the coastal fields in the evening-time. They were beautiful birds, too, with a greenish sheen on their wings and a distinctive plume on their heads. Their haunting call was one of the commonest sounds of the countryside round our cottage.

Land and sea were vital and vibrant influences on the lives of all of us.

My father died suddenly one fine March evening, when the daffodils were swaying along the ditches of the field and the flowers of the wild currant were wine-red in the hedgerow. Later that summer my brother, who became a member of the fishing crew at the age of eleven, brought home the first salmon of the season. When my mother saw the salmon, lying fresh and silvery on the small cold floor of the porch, she cried bitter-sweet tears of sadness and remembrance. 'Paddy used love the silvery salmon,' she said aloud, as if no one was listening at all.

It was the end of a childhood.

2
Friends and Neighbours

As children we never stratified people into classes, but even our unobservant eyes could distinguish at least four different social groups in the countryside where we lived.

At the top of the scale was the Marshall family who owned the great country house close by our cottage, represented when I was a child by Mrs. Ruth, a daughter of the house. Most people regarded her with a certain awe and she stood apart from the local people, not only in matters of land and religion but also because of her sometimes intimidating Anglo-Irish accent. But there was nothing aloof about her; she was keenly interested in community affairs and an active member of the local Muintir na Tire guild, which in pioneering fashion organised the building of the parish hall in Milltown in the fifties.

On the next rung of the ladder came the big farmers, who owned sizeable acreages of land and employed farm workers on a regular basis, extra men being hired during the busy sowing and harvesting periods. The big farmers in Callinafercy were the Langfords, the Kellihers and the O'Sullivans, the latter being known as the Quart Sullivans to distinguish them from other families of the same name.

The third group was the small farmers who worked their small holdings themselves or with the help of neighbours. Then there were the labourers, such as my father, who might own a tiny field or garden and nothing more, and who worked for farmers or for the County Council on the roads or for the Board of Works on the river banks.

Hiring fairs were held in Killorglin until the 1930s. Young men like my uncles would stand at the corners with their spades and shovels, hoping to be hired from February to October, the customary period in these parts. There was even a song about them which we learned at school—*An Spailpín Fánach*—about the wandering labourers, who went from parish to parish and county to county, in search of work, rather as students today go to pick hops or fruit in countries overseas at, hopefully, higher rates of pay.

Some lines of that poem still linger in my memory:

> Oh, come let us go,
> For the road is long.
> Come away with the *Spailpín Fánach*.

Long hours and low wages were very much the norm for the farm labourer in those days. Many were the stories we heard about that life from our aunts and uncles, who had worked for farmers in the twenties before they emigrated to America. Two of my aunts, Mary and Nora, had to milk six to eight cattle by hand, morning and evening, and they were also required to feed the calves, pigs and poultry. The rest of their day was spent doing housework, making meals, washing clothes and looking after the farmer's children. One of our neighbours told us that when he worked on a farm in the forties he had to rise at five o'clock in the morning and the day's work normally continued until nine at night. Because of the long hours they usually slept in, often, as in the case of Aunt Mary, in a tiny room or loft at the very top of the farmhouse. They got a few days off at Christmas but seldom returned home for the remainder of the year.

The social distinction between big farmer and farm labourer was sharply defined. The 'servant boys and girls' took their meals apart from the family, and in one farmhouse a single plate was allotted to every two labourers, with a small piece of bacon, cabbage and potatoes on one side for one man, the same on the other side for the second man, a custom which continued up until the late thirties.

St. Brigid's Day had a special significance, as Bob Knightly explained to me:

> Before Biddy's Day, the farm workers would get two males (meals) a day. After Biddy's Day they'd get three. That's why we had this saying in Callinafercy: 'Welcome, Biddy, and your three-male day'.

Since money was scarce it had sometimes been the custom for the labourer to give his labour free to the farmer for a day or two in return for various concessions such as the loan of a donkey and cart to bring home turf from the bog, or as payment for the use of a tiny plot of land which belonged to the farmer. We were given a few drills of potatoes on the Marshall estate. We had to supply the seed ourselves and in return we were generally expected to help to pick the estate potatoes in September, an arrangement we always considered quite fair. The day of the potato picking was very much a social gathering, with pickers coming from far and near.

In general, however, casual labour was not exactly a piece of cake. One Callinafercy man summed it up somewhat caustically: 'You'd work from dawn to dusk for the farmer and the sweat'd be dropping off you, but all you'd get in the evening was "The Lord spare you the health".'

If the conditions in those days sound harsh, it must be remembered that most farmers fared badly during the economic depression of the thirties. My grandfather, we were told, had a cow for sale and was offered five shillings for the animal—this seemed to be the going rate at Killorglin fairs in 1931 and 1932. The labouring classes of Callinafercy were, however, more fortunate than others in many respects in that they were close to both the rivers Laune and Maine, both teeming with highly prized salmon. Most survived on a combination of small scale farming, labouring and fishing, a pattern which still existed in the early sixties. From then on, living conditions improved, and industry, represented by a few small local factories, offered new and hitherto unknown prospects for employment.

Naturally, given the social conditions, one of the most important members of the country community was the local shopkeeper. There had been a grocery shop on the bog road, owned by Maggie Shea, but when we were children another shop was opened, near the new main road linking

Milltown and Killorglin. It was owned by Timmy Kennedy, whose father had been a shoemaker, and it stocked a large selection of everything anyone round about might need, for animals and poultry as well as themselves. Oils of various kinds; wellington boots; farm implements; bags of potatoes; sweets such as bull's eyes and cloves and lozenges in big glass jars; groceries like sugar that had to be weighed into brown paper bags, and bacon that was cut according to the customer's need.

As we had potatoes and cabbage from our own little garden, we were self-sufficient to some extent, but there were often times during the winter when my mother, in common with most of the households around, was forced to buy food on credit until my father's pay-day at the week-end. As he worked as a labourer on the roads or the river banks his wages were very low, so my mother made a rule that credit should never exceed a certain amount. Purchasing groceries on credit or on tick was politely referred to by the shopkeeper as 'being in the book', since he noted down all such transactions in a big red ledger. My mother often worried about being in debt, no matter how small the amount owed, and she frequently went about the house saying, 'I'll have to pay what's in the book now on Saturday.' But the shopkeeper was lenient when it came to payment and no interest was ever charged.

We fared better during the summer months when the salmon season brought with it an inflow of badly needed income.

Like most of the women in the area, my mother believed that a family would never go totally broke if a coin of any kind was placed under a statue of the Infant Jesus of Prague; no other statue was acceptable. Luckily my father had won such a statue at a bazaar at Puck Fair, and there was usually an old sixpence placed beneath it to ensure that the family finances would never sink too low for too long. My mother also kept a solitary twenty-pound note wrapped in a small

paper bag—never to be used except in the direst emergency—
and that old note gave us all a warm feeling of financial
security. No emergency must ever have been thought dire
enough for its use—because I still have it!

The country people I knew when I was growing up were
colourful interesting people, with lifestyles differing radically
from those who live in Kerry today. Life was lived at a
leisurely pace. Farming was less intensive and viewed more
as a way of life than a business venture where the books
had to balance at the end of the day. I remember the older
people as being full of merry wit and poetry, and in the
days before radio and television they had, in fact, composed
their own songs about local events. I often heard my
grandmother tell how the men would, in the absence of
chairs, sit or lie on the tiny kitchen floor 'making songs
into the early hours of the morning'. The storm might rage
outside but inside there was warmth and cheerfulness and
congenial conversation. Even today these old songs have
an astonishing spontaneity and wit.

Many of the older generation had a quick wit. One old
neighbour, Dan, on a return visit to the optician to enquire
about his wife's new glasses, mentioned that there seemed
to be a very long delay.

'I'm not a miracle worker,' snapped the optician. 'Do
you think I'm God Almighty or what?'

'At the rate you're operating, isn't it a blessin' to the
rest of us that you're not,' answered Dan.

One quartet of old people lived in an ivy-covered
farmhouse, fronted by a garden and an orchard and a low-
trimmed hedge, which lay at the end of a long narrow lane
known as the factory; so-called because a shirt factory had
been sited here in the waning years of the nineteenth century.
There was always a warm welcome from Joan, Bob, Maggie
and Kate, and one would be ushered into the kitchen with
its old-fashioned dresser laden with beautiful cups and jugs.

The shelf above the hearth held a variety of tins and groceries such as sugar which were susceptible to the damp, there was a brash red bin for storing flour and meal, and from the wall came the lazy tick of the pendulum clock. Indeed every country kitchen at that time seemed to have a wall clock made by the Anglo-American Wall Clock Company.

The family were noted dog breeders and the love and tenderness lavished on the family dogs by Joan and Bob was truly remarkable. They were treated not as pets but as honoured companions. A special chair was reserved for Sheila, the much-revered mother of a long line of handsome brown-and-white sheepdogs. The furry little pups often romped and played about the cement floor of the kitchen but when things became a little too boisterous, Joan would instantly shout, 'Sheila, up on your chair!' The well trained sheepdog would immediately return to her place of honour and order would be restored. The talk was usually about the dogs: How a man had travelled all the way from North Kerry for one of Sheila's celebrated progeny; how a certain sheep farmer had found another pup to be the most intelligent and obedient dog he had ever trained; how a woman had been broken-hearted when her old sheepdog died and she had come begging for another. On one occasion Bob consented to give us one of a litter of those precious pups and when the time came to part with the fluffy little dog, he held it lovingly in his hands and stroked its back saying, 'Another little man going away!' Generally in those days there was a great affinity between country people and their animals. It was not uncommon for cows, sheep, even hens and geese, to be given names as a gesture of friendship and kindness.

Joan and Bob were very proud of the geese, which wandered through the farmyard and the fields at the back of the house in a massive flock, inevitably headed by the protective and aggressive gander. As a child I thought that geese were noisy clumsy birds, and yet they held a strange fascination for me. The very size of their eggs made them objects of interest, and often, when a conversation was in mid-stream, Joan would interject with sudden alarm, 'Hey, Bob, did that goose lay yet?' In between the chat and the banter, the work of the house went on. Joan, in her traditional bib, would make her flat cakes of soda bread on the griddle on the open fire; Bob would milk the cows in the eveningtime and Joan would fill a bottle for us straight from the bucket, and so we took home with us 'a bottle of the finest milk in Callinafercy'. It was always with regret that we said good-bye to Joan and Bob and their exuberant family of dogs and geese.

Another old neighbour had a crafty way of dealing with awkward questions which might be concerned with secret or sensitive information. As she listened intently to the latest details of local gossip her hearing would be perfect. But whenever asked a question herself that she chose not to answer, she would peer vaguely and heedlessly into the distance, as if she had not heard a single syllable that had just been uttered. The question could be repeated but the old woman's hearing would appear to be beyond repair— for a few moments at least—until someone else volunteered a few titbits of information on some subject; then miraculously her hearing would return.

One of the most pleasant experiences of my childhood was visiting a neighbour who lived close by in a whitewashed cottage, which had a tiny garden alive with colour and fragrance. Jack was a great man for the flowers, everyone said, and he was also the proud owner of an old-fashioned gramophone, which came complete with a shining trumpet-shaped horn. He had an extensive collection of old seventy-eight records, mainly traditional favourites, all of which were neatly stored in separate blue sleeves in a plum-coloured folder. Both gramophone and records could be quite temperamental at times. Indeed they seemed to have a will of their own. Long hours were regularly spent placing them at a discreet distance from the fire as we attempted 'to dry the dampness out of them'. There was a great sense of anticipation when the old man finally turned the gramophone handle and gently placed the long, pointed needle on the record. Songs like *Down by the Sally Garden* and *The Star of the County Down*— and of course *The Kerry Dances*—were played again and again, but our favourite was Jimmy O'Dea; Biddy Mulligan was, and always will be in our hearts, the pride of the Coombe.

The advance of technology, however, soon enabled us to go one better. The introduction of electricity in 1956 was shortly followed by the arrival of a radio—always referred to as the wireless in our house. Ours was an old-fashioned Mullard radio, which was given pride of place on a shelf in the kitchen. It was customary for some of the neighbours to drop in on a Sunday afternoon, and everyone would listen excitedly to the commentary on some important game. Our neighbour, Mary, was wont to bang the table with her hands at regular intervals when anyone scored a goal; it didn't seem to matter whether the goal was scored by Kerry or their opponents. It was well into the year 1965 before a black and white TV arrived in a neighbour's house, and now the games could be seen as well as heard. Sometimes when the Kerry team arrived on to the pitch Mary in her confusion would say, 'Wisha, how will our Kerry boys play them big, long, lanky divils at all?'

I vividly remember Annie Sullivan's thatched house, which we often visited on our way to or from Bob Knightly's. The walls were painted with a solution of yellow ochre and lime, and the garden wall was also painted yellow, with the top in a light shade of blue that echoed the blue of the gate, the door and the little window frames. There were masses of hydrangeas in the garden and deep-pink roses, deliciously scented, scrambled about the walls. Miss Twiss, a frequent visitor to Mrs. Ruth, was so enchanted by Annie's house that she painted two wonderful little cameos of it, presenting one of them to Annie herself.

Annie's niece, Eileen Murphy, told me about the dances that were held in the houses in earlier days:

> They'd have a dance in her house on a Saturday night. My mother Debbie played the melodeon, Jack Leary the concertina and there were good fiddlers too. They'd have tea and barmbrack and the people that came sometimes gave her a few pence to pay for expenses. Now and then they went round with the Biddy and afterwards they had a ball night. My aunt was a good singer and when they used go into old Mrs Lambe, Jamsie Lambe's (the teacher) mother, Annie used sing *Kevin Barry*. She was great for singing *Kevin Barry* and Mrs Lambe used say, 'Good, Annie, good.' Then they'd go back to Marshall's big house (Callinafercy) and dance the half-set and Kathleen the cook would give them tea and brack.

I myself remember Annie as an old and gentle woman, the tick of the pendulum clock on the wall making music with the drone of the bees in the garden beyond, as she made tea for me and my mother. In her young days, she had done general housework for the Williams of Callinafercy House. She had also worked for the Reids, another Protestant family, 'washing and doing the barrelling', the latter being an old country way of describing the making of butter, and in the springtime she cut the seed-potatoes at the home of the Marshalls.

Mary and her husband Jer lived in a thatched house, with roses and lilacs and a very distinctive snowball tree in the front garden. He was adept at making chairs and tables and most houses in the locality had samples of his handiwork. He was very much afraid of ghosts, a weakness exploited by a few of the local jokers who once tied two pieces of string to his shoes beside the bed and, by tugging the strings, moved the shoes slowly and deliberately across the floor.

Mary declared that 'poor Jer was fit for the priest after um'. He was a kind-hearted man and when he returned from town he invariably brought with him a paper bag of edible mice—white and pink —which could be purchased for a penny each and which he distributed to the neighbours' children. A visit to Killorglin was a big event for young and old alike at that time, so naturally we were always around to welcome him home from town.

Mary wore a blue knitted cardigan and blouse over an old black skirt. Her navy coat and navy straw hat were reserved for special occasions such as funerals and weddings and visits to town. She had been in America many years before (no one quite knew when; she was extremely reluctant to disclose her age and became suitably offended if anyone suggested she might be old) and delighted in recalling what she called 'shore parties', where a group of young men and women had a party beside the sea. She was, she told us, a big hit with the men, who always said she had a roving eye. Sometimes she forgot the names of places, telling American visitors that she used to live 'not far from that big square where they park the cars'. After further clues and much detective work the location of the square would be at last identified and the riddle solved. Mary's language contained many Americanisms, a deliberate policy to impress. We children were never cheeky; always too fresh. She would relate how she had seen a familiar face in town and how she had 'hollored' over to them. Indeed her occasional forays into the town of Killorglin were the joy of her life and provided fodder for conversation for many weeks afterwards.

One of her favourite activities was making buttermilk in her little black teapot. She shook the tiny pot vigorously and, with no little skill, dipping in her finger from time to time to check the texture of the liquid, ended up with genuine buttermilk. She often came to visit us, and whenever she was offered a cup of tea she would invariably reply,

'Ereh, I'll have wan sup in the bottom of the cup.' She was known for the heartiness of her appetite and was very partial to boiled nettles, which she regularly ate for medicinal purposes. One of the local wags suggested, 'If you gave that wan a pike of briars she'd ate um for you.' She became something of a celebrity when some of her money was stolen. Robberies were unknown in those days and doors were seldom locked, so the theft of Mary's nest-egg was an event of some consequence. The local guards went through the formalities of knocking on doors, asking if people had any information on the subject, but the money was never recovered. In the heat of the moment, Mary, who would not have harmed a fly, was heard to express the wish that the robbers 'might hang and hang high'.

In wintertime the swollen river often burst through the banks, flooding the fields and sweeping furiously down the narrow road. Our house, high on the hill, was safe from the rising waters, but Jer and Mary's little thatched cottage lay directly in their path. At those times a fishing boat was dispatched down along the road, the men rowing with a feverish kind of earnestness in the bid to rescue the stranded pair and their precious belongings. It was quite an operation, as other low-lying households also had to be rescued.

Another neighbour who was regularly flooded out was Dan Linehan. He lived at the store (the site of a former grain store), a cottage built right on the edge of the tide. He seemed to accept this philosophically, pointing out the watermark on the wall with a certain relish, comparing it with the levels that had been reached on previous occasions. The joy of his life were the little goldfinches he kept in cages. They filled his kitchen with vibrant colour and melodious warbling right through the day.

One local character wore a coarse bag on his head whenever it rained, and he sometimes wore his vest outside his shirt in the summertime. He was always seeing ghosts or Jackie-the-lantern or the great black dog of Callinafercy, and on stormy nights as we sat round the cottage fire he told and retold stories of the many strange sights he had seen, stories which often frightened the wits out of us children when we were sent off to our beds and the darkness closed in around us. There was one pleasant story, however, which I always tried to keep in the forefront of my mind when less pleasant thoughts intruded. One frosty moonlit Christmas Eve, beneath star-studded heavens that were hushed and silent, he had seen a mysterious flock of sheep grazing in a leisurely fashion in a field on the cliff-top beside the river. Nothing would convince him that they were an illusion, although no trace of the fantastic flock could be found the next day. That was one story I hoped was true and not just the figment of a fertile imagination.

In autumn he went about with a few small apples in his trouser pockets and these would be presented to us, after a period of weeks, when he considered they had matured sufficiently within the pockets. He had strange ideas about food; cornflakes, which made their appearance on our table in the sixties, should be steeped overnight so that they might lose their crispness.

Minor feuds between families were commonplace, so while my friend and I were allowed to pick blackberries in his field, he chased the child of a feuding neighbour off his land with a pitchfork. For some inexplicable reason, in spite of his Christmas Eve vision, he had always hated sheep farmers—sheep were 'contrary devils'—and when my sister began to go out with the son of a sheep farmer this increased his hostility towards 'them blashted mountainy men'. My sister was something of a favourite with him; the flower of the cliff he called her. She often teased him in a good-humoured way, asking him if he would leave her a field when he died; the response was always vague and the field never materialised. He cried and cried when he heard that she was emigrating to America for a few years.

There were other neighbours, too, that I remember with

fondness. Jer Tim, another fisherman, was very adept at making fine rushwork crosses for St. Brigid's Day. Tadg Harmon and his sister Mary lived in a thatched house beside the river, and it was a familiar sight to see him returning to the strand with a boat-load of reeds. Another Harmon, Hannah, worked at Caragh Cliff, a modest house over at Caragh Lake. It was occupied at that time by Mr and Mrs Ruth, and Hannah vividly recalled them playing croquet on the lawn. Sometimes, when they were away for the day, the three servants—cook, housemaid and gardener—would try their hand at this unfamiliar sport. Mr. Ruth often went fishing—they shared a boat with one of the neighbours— and he spent a lot of his time out of the house. One of his characteristics, according to Hannah, was that he was always whistling: 'When you'd hear the whistle you'd know he was coming.'

Mick Murphy was known locally as Mickeen Seán Dubh, and a friend of his had a still more colourful nickname— Pickee Ó! Mickeen Seán Dubh was a great one for the stories and his favourite was about the War of Independence. One night he and Pickee Ó! were in a neighbouring house when the Black and Tans burst in through the front door. The lads escaped through the back door and took to the fields. They ran and ran, crossing gates and hedges along the way. At length they jumped across a ditch in Reid's farm and Pickee Ó! had the misfortune to half land on a calf that was lying on the ground. The calf gave a roar as it staggered to its feet, and the fugitives almost died of fright. They ran on, even faster than before, and they had gone a considerable distance before they realised that the roar had come from the calf and not from some supernatural being on the prowl. In his youth, Mickeen sold apples for a farmer. The apples were picked one day and the next day Mickeen, having left his own home at five o'clock in the morning, took them to Cahirciveen by pony and trap. Here he sold them door to door.

My mother's best friend was None Sullivan, and they often made a point of sitting beside each other at a station mass in a local house. Among her other friends were Sheila McKenna, Lizzie McKenna, Mary Sullivan, Betty Clifford, Dote Sullivan and Nancy Murphy; occasionally one or other came in for a pair of curtains that my mother made on her prized sewing machine.

Rivalry of a friendly kind between neighbouring townlands was very much an aspect of life in the fifties. Callinafercy and nearby Steelroe, for instance, both depended on fishing for their livelihood, the former on the Maine, the latter on the Laune. The local poets added fuel to the fire by composing rhymes such as:

> Hay and oats for the Steelroe goats;
> Eggs and rashers for the Callinfercy dashers.

The words Steelroe and Callinafercy could, of course, be interchanged in the rhyme according to discretion.

My aunt Mag and her husband lived in the farmhouse on the Marshall estate. She made home-made butter in a barrel churn and it was usual to see her busy at it when we called on them. When the butter had come, she sometimes gave us cups of buttermilk, which we drank with great relish. She also looked after the hens and the flock of Muscovy ducks, large greenish-black ducks with a conspicuous red carbuncle on the bill. Like my mother, she made a cake of fresh soda bread every day in the pot oven. Her husband's job was tending the black Kerry cattle which were such a distinctive feature of the landscape at that time.

Her dresser, which she told me she had purchased for thirty shillings in the mid-forties, differed from ours in that the superstructure of shelves was supported, not by a press, but by two drawers above an open base, where large pots and pans were stored behind neatly sewn hangings of furniture cotton. She remembered housewives going to town a few weeks before Christmas to buy a piece of new furniture cotton for the dresser 'hangings'.

Aunt Mag had the old country habit of cross-indexing dates and events. Thus a story about a neighbour's boat would be made even more memorable in her mind because it coincided with a family birth. Reminiscing one day, she began:

> On July 14, 1906, when my sister Nora was born, Jimín the Store's big boat was anchored over near Ballykissane. Jimín's boat had a big sail and he used sail over to Inch and places, drawing home loads of sand for the farmers around Callinafercy. This particular night, a very wild night, Ger M. and another lad unfurled the sail. The fine sail was swept away by the wind but the boat couldn't move because 'twas anchored firmly. There was a court case afterwards when Jimín brought the lads to court.

Another aunt, Kathy, also lived nearby. Her husband Bill was an excellent fiddle player and was much sought after by those who appreciated good music. She had her own

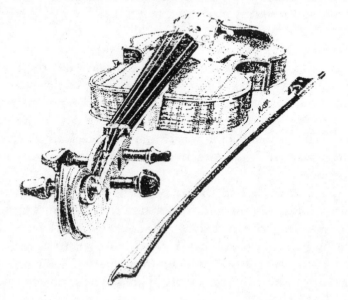

store of old customs and traditions. My mother might believe that the statue of the Infant Jesus of Prague ensured financial security; my aunt knew that if the same statue was placed outside the door during the night, the next day was sure to be fine. She also believed that it was unlucky for a child, a parent and a grandparent, bearing the same Christian name, to live in the same house.

Aunt Mary Anne usually came to visit us in the summertime, and whenever she came the talk was always of old childhood days in the farmhouse by the stream at Claodach. She lived in a picturesque cottage not far from Holy Cross Abbey in County Tipperary. Like my mother, she was a great lover of flowers and had them in pots all around her house; she was also an expert knitter.

The returned Yank was a phenomenon of those early summers, and when my Aunt Nora wrote to say that she was coming to Ireland in a few weeks' time her letter caused a stir of excitement amongst family and friends. My mother insisted on cleaning the house from top to bottom. If anyone tried to persuade her that it was perfectly all right as it was, she would say knowingly, 'You know how fussy Yanks are .'

It was a fine summer's evening in July when I returned home from school to find that the Yank had finally arrived. Aunt Nora—hair dyed auburn-brown, pink lipstick shimmering on her lips—sat at the top of the table, while the aroma of freshly made coffee filled the kitchen. She wore a bright pink dress with a bold floral pattern, and two eye-catching earrings dangled from her ear lobes. She was then sixty-two years old but she looked much younger. She drew me towards her, hugged me tightly, kissed me on the cheek and presented me with a silvery coin as a present. There followed an incessant gush of speech in a pronounced American accent. One of the things I remember her saying was that life in Ireland was much better now

because 'at least you don't have to leave school at fifteen
to go workin' for the farmer'. What funny shoes Yanks
wore, I thought, as I looked at her pink sandals, which
were strapless at the back and decorated with embroidered
gilt designs round the toes!

During the next few days I was to discover that everything
in America was much better and bigger and brighter than
in Ireland. While she treated the neighbours to highballs
and whiskey sours, she proudly proclaimed the greatness
of the USA. She also loved the idea of 'riding' in the donkey
and cart to collect the fish, even though she often made
remarks about her aching backside that made me giggle and
titter. She loved talking about the old days—the twenties—
'when the men came in and they'd lie on the floor because
we didn't have enough chairs, and they'd make up songs
and poems about the fishing, sprinkled here and there with
a few unsavoury jibes at the water bailiffs.' Then there would
be a hearty laugh as she relived her memories of other days.
The fish often attracted flies which swarmed round the
donkey, and she spent a great deal of her time trying to
'swat those damned insects'. She was a great one for
socialising and during her visit I saw more of Kerry than
I had seen in the whole of my previous existence. She was
rarely satisfied with half measures, and so when we toured
the Ring of Kerry we took half the locality with us, in
a minibus that had been specially hired for the purpose.
Insomnia was one of her favourite complaints, though when
she took her regular afternoon nap the tiles on the roof
almost rattled with the sound of her snores. 'And that's
the wan that doesn't sleep a wink,' my mother would say
with a grin.

If we had considered that my mother was fastidious about
cleanliness, we soon discovered that the Yank was even
worse. 'When she's not washing herself, she's washing her
shirt,' my father often said. She dragged the big tin bath
into her bedroom and I hurried about with kettles of hot

water. She was a great lover, too, of blazing turf fires, even in the middle of summer; she 'just couldn't stand the dampness, honey'.

I liked Aunt Nora very much. She was different—she was fun. Not surprisingly there were tears in my eyes when she was returning to the States. After my father's death, she visited us again, this time with Aunt Mary and Aunt Mary's husband, Johnny Grandfield, who hailed originally from the Dingle area. Aunt Mary suffered greatly from arthritis but this did not deter her from travelling in the donkey and cart, which she struggled into with the aid of her walking cane and an old timber butter box. It was Aunt Mary who had, in the 1930s, sent from America the money which paid for the very fine Celtic cross which still stands over the grave of her parents, my grandparents. Her husband was a wonderfully gentle easy-going man. He loved talking with the neighbours and taking the occasional drink. He was very fond of animals, especially the donkey, and he was more than happy to help with the lifting of the fish into the cart. Sometimes he had trouble understanding Mrs. Ruth's accent, which made me smile. Of course Aunt Nora was very polite to Mrs. Ruth but when the great lady took her leave of us, her much-loved terriers might be jocosely dismissed as 'a pack of old flea bags'.

Travellers or tinkers called regularly in those days but they were expecially plentiful during Puck Fair in Killorglin. They travelled in brightly coloured horse-drawn caravans and they were rarely fussy about where their piebald horses decided to graze during the night. The women usually came to the door weighed down with baskets of holy pictures, statues, medals, relics, and even pieces of scented cloth that had been rubbed against some relic or other in Rome. Whenever they were given a small donation they showered down blessings on everything and everyone in the house—even the dog and cat got a mention at times. They could however be very persistent. When they had been given some home-made bread, they invariably asked for a small *tasteen* of butter. When a few spoonfuls of tea had been filled into a paper bag, they vowed they would pray for us till kingdom come if they could only have a few hampfuls of sugar to go with it.

The language used by country people was very much a *meascán* or mixture of Irish and English. When things did not go her way my grandmother had a store of less than savoury phrases to call upon. These included *Hanam an diabhail* ('Your soul to the devil'), *File scrain ort* and *Masla chugat*, both of which, loosely translated, mean 'Bad luck to you'. She also made use of the more reverent *Dia linn go deo* ('God with us forever').

If my father happened to find a missing needle or tack on the floor he would solemnly announce that it was the will of God he found it, for if he had stepped on it, he would have got an awful *mácail*, a word which means wound. A neighbour might come to borrow a *taoscán* (a little quantity) of tay, while if anyone asked for a third or fourth cup of tea they would surely be told that was only *dríodar* (dregs) in the pot now. A silly old woman who was always rushing hither and thither was unflatteringly described as 'that *ainniseoir* (miserable person) that's ever in a *fústar* (rush)'. Beggar women were said to be full of *plámas* (flattery), while they in turn encouraged the householder to be a bit more *flaithiúil* (generous).

When a neighbour made a bad purchase or struck a bad bargain, my father might declare sarcastically, 'That lad have no more sense than a *faoileáin* (seagull).' Noisy children— which we were—were often berated as being *clamparsome* (difficult, noisy) divils. Someone who seemed to be making too much of an effort to be pleasant was said to be all *grá-mo-chroi* (literally, love of my heart). A man who walked with a waddle was a *lapadóir* (waddler); a slovenly creature was a *slapadóir* (untidy person), while someone who was always misplacing things was an awful *útamálai* (bungler). If I dropped a cup on the floor my mother might declare disconsolately that it was in *brúscar* (fragments), advising me to clean it up quickly or my father would make *raic* (quarrel, noise).

My uncle Donal had his own favourite Irish expressions. People who boasted of their exploits were, he said, full of *gaisce* (literally the word means great deeds but here it conveyed boastfulness) or were all *saothair* (work, endeavour). When we went to his house to have our hair cut with the hand machine—we went to the barber only on rare occasions—he usually chided us for going about so long with such a *mothail* (mop) of hair on our heads.

3
The Land and its Traditions

The River Maine is one of the most beautiful features of the Milltown landscape. A Victorian guide-book gives a vivid description of it 'rising suddenly from a well called *Tobar Mang*' near Castleisland. When the Normans arrived in Kerry, they regarded the river as the dividing line between the new Anglo-Norman world and the old Gaelic order, the frontier between their own newly acquired territories and those of the McCarthy Mór, the Moriarties and the O'Sullivans—the original native Irish clans.

A line of Norman castles soon appeared along the rivers Maine and Laune, the most important being that of Castle-maine, which was built by Maurice Fitzgerald in 1215; he also established a stronghold at Callinafercy a few years later. Other Norman castles in the vicinity were Killorglin (1215) and Castleisland, which was erected in 1226 by Geoffrey de Maurisco, the King's Justiciar in Ireland. Castlemaine Castle remained in the possession of the Fitzmaurice family until the great Desmond Rebellion (1569-73). The castle was besieged by Sir John Perrott, the Lord President of Munster, in 1572. A document records that 'a curious plan or picture of the siege lies in the State Paper Office; it represents the old fortress on the bridge; in a field before it are two large cannons, volumes of smoke issuing from their mouths; close by stands the Abbey of Killagha, not yet ruined, but between it and the President's camp stands a tall gallows.' The Desmond Rebellion was utterly crushed, and the castle changed hands several times over the next eighty years, surviving intact until the triumph of Ludlow's Cromwellian forces in the year 1652. Then it fell into ruin.

The policy of 'planting' conquered land with loyal English Protestant settlers had begun during the reigns of Elizabeth I and James I, but it was Cromwell's Act of Settlement of 1652 that was the real watershed in land ownership in the Milltown area. It laid down that 'all delinquent landowners' (those who had supported the Rebellion of 1641 and had later opposed Cromwell) were 'to be removed across the Shannon to Connaught, where they were to receive lands equivalent in value to that portion of their estates which they were legally entitled to retain.' Under the terms of the Act, the province of Connaught was to include the county of Clare and it was to West Clare that the original owners of the lands of Milltown were sent, some months before the arrival of Colonel John Godfrey in 1656.

The Colonel was granted an estate of 4,980 acres in Kerry, which included almost every townland in the vicinity of Milltown. The Act also granted to him and his descendants the fishing rights on the River Laune—a privilege which the family claimed and exploited well into the twentieth century. After Cromwell's death, the Godfreys not only retained their estates; they received fresh grants of land from Charles II, principally the Abbey of Killagha. The Abbey was built around the year 1215, probably on the site of the Irish monastery of Kilcoleman, by Geoffrey de Maurisco, for the Order of the Canons Regular of St. Augustine. It was heavily endowed with lands and tithes which were, at the dissolution of the monasteries in 1576, granted to Captain Spring (the Springs had come to Kerry in the 1500s) but were forfeited by him because of his part in the Rebellion of 1641. After the Restoration of Charles II, the rectory was assigned to the family of Lord Ventry, but the Abbey, with all its riches, was granted to the Godfrey family. Interestingly, this monastic connection is strong in local memories.

Charles II has another link with the area. In 1660 he took a fancy to Barbara Villiers, a nineteen-year-old beauty with rich auburn hair and blue eyes, and a child was duly born. She was married to a Roger Palmer, described as 'an obscure person, who was the father of not one of his wife's numerous offspring'. But as 'Mrs Palmer' was hardly a suitable title for a King's mistress, he was created Earl of Castlemaine, and Countess of Castlemaine she remained until she was promoted to be Duchess of Cleveland nine years later. Why the king chose Castlemaine, which didn't even have a castle to its name at this stage, is uncertain. There is no record that she ever came to look over her domain.

Under Cromwell's Act of Settlement, Colonel Godfrey was required to settle a large number of English Protestants on his estates and he soon began fulfilling this obligation. The first families arrived in the waning years of the seventeenth century and they included such names as Allman, Conyers, Dumas, Giles, Harmon, Jeffcott, Langtry, Langford, Myles, Neville, Peneton, Ridley, Stephens, Twiss, Wren and West. Three hundred years later, only a few of these family names survive in the parish, though some of them are still to be found elsewhere in Kerry. The Myles family is remembered for the fact that they owned the 'haunted house' of Callinafercy, while a certain Captain Jeffcott is said to have been the first to acquire a set of false teeth in the locality, at a time when such objects were 'the eighth wonder of the world'.

The original tenants probably thrived for a time but there were simply not enough of them to farm the vast Godfrey estates. New tenants were needed, not only to work the land but also to provide the landowner with more and more rent. So, the native Irish appeared again on the lands of Kilcoleman in the eighteenth century. They came from all parts of Munster. Sullivans and Sheas travelled from the Iveragh peninsula. Cronins and Barretts came from Cork, Heffernans and Hanafins from Tipperary, while the McKennas came from even further afield—from County Monaghan. The transplantation to Connaught was only partially successful in the case of certain families; the McCarthys and Moriarties returned and found themselves a place in the new scheme of things.

The other great landlord family, the Marshalls of Callinafercy, also had English roots, having come to Ireland with the expedition led by Sir Charles Wilmot in 1602. The Marshalls intermarried with the Markhams, another Cromwellian family, and later with the Godfreys, acquiring in that manner very handsome estates in Kerry.

Some attempts were made by the planters and their landlords to change the native Irish place-names but these efforts failed miserably. Virtually all the townlands still retain their Irish names or English corruptions of them. The native Irish did, in fact, name their fields with considerable accuracy and the names of fields around Milltown, still in use in the fifties, provide a vivid and vibrant link with the events of yester-year. *Pairc na Soupers* in Callinafercy recalls the famine soup kitchens; the peninsula of *Rinn Scolathan* (peninsula of the school) the existence of a nearby Protestant school in the not-too-distant past. The name of the adjacent field has an ominous ring to it— *Gort na Cnamh* (the field of the bones). Another field was known as *Pairc na Scoile* because sometime between 1830 and 1840 a hedge school had been established there. It was apparently built against one of the ditches and covered with rushes, a part of the building also serving as the home of the schoolmaster. His name was Michael O'Connell, and it was believed that he was a relative of Daniel O'Connell the liberator. *Pairc na Fuil*, the field of blood, commemorates some long forgotten battle, while *Garrai an Oir*, the garden of gold, was the name given to a field famous for its wheat crops.

Fields were often named after their first tenants. When the Marshalls came to Callinafercy, for instance, they rented out fields which very often had to be cleared of scrub and furze and briars. One such field was rented to Tadgh Mór Heffernan, who cut away all the furze in the field and developed it into good agricultural land; generations later the field was still known as Tadgh Mór's. A large field of some seventy acres on the Godfrey estate was known as the *Albanach*:

' 'Twas how the Godfreys brought over some kind of an agricultural adviser from Scotland. His name was Evans and he made great changes. The old people said that 'twas Evans brought in turnips and mangolds to Milltown for the very first time. He brought in new breeds of cattle and sheep too but the locals didn't take to them for years. The *Albanach* field was called after Evans the Scot.

The Godfreys are also credited with introducing a new variety of furze, from France, to the Milltown area:

There was an Irish furze here before they came and 'twas just call *aiteann*, but when the Godfreys brought in the French furze, the Irish furze became known as *aiteann Gaelach* and the French one *aiteann Gallda*.

Furze was an important crop in Kerry. When Charles Etienne Coquebert de Montbert visited many parts of the county in 1790, he noted that furze, which was regarded with contempt in other countries, played a positive role in the rural economy of Kerry. Wood was so scarce that furze was used as fuel, and also for cooking purposes by the poorer households. The buds of specially cultivated furze were cut and crushed and fed to farm animals including horses, the latter preferring it to oats. My mother often told us that that in her youth it was customary for small farmers to supplement the diet of cattle with finely chopped furze.

Milltown's linen industry is commemorated in Rawley's field (called after a one-time owner of the mills), Bleach Road and Bleach Lane. There is, however, some doubt about the origin of the 'hospital' field, two hundred yards from the village of Milltown. One tradition associates it with the monks of Killagha Abbey, who were supposed to have established a house for the treatment of leprosy, a term which was then applied to a variety of skin diseases; in the state papers of 1583 there is a note which says that 'the house of lepers between Killagha and Killorglin is nearly wasted'. Another tradition suggests that a hospital was built in the field in the early 1840s under the direction of the local parish priest, Father Quill. A group of sailors suffering from cholera visited Tralee port about that time, on board a large merchant vessel which was delivering goods at the quay. The disease spread rapidly and a large number of people in Milltown caught the infection. According to the story, the hospital at Tralee was unable to cope with the numbers, so a small hospital was erected near Milltown, in the 'hospital' field.

Just how far back folk memories can go is illustrated by the name, the orchard field, which adjoins Killagha Abbey; this was where the monks established their fruit gardens sometime around 1215.

The local fairies also had their favourite fields. A great hole in the earth near Milltown, *Poll Dearg*, is supposed to have been the work of a fairy woman who took the earth away in her apron and let it fall some distance from Killorglin; the place where she emptied the contents of her apron was known as *Cnocan Ard Dearg*, the high red hill. And as children we were proud, if sometimes a little fearful, of our association with the *sidhe*—the field in which our cottage was built was where the fairy teams of Callinafercy played their late night football games.

'To everything there is a season. A time for sowing; a time for reaping.' We did not have to be told this; as season followed season, so did the sowing, the harvesting and the various rural activities that were part of life in rural Ireland.

The practice of planting a small garden continued well into the fifties and sixties. My father cut the seed potatoes into two halves or *sceallains*, making sure that each had an eye for growth. They were planted with a spade in rows of three, in carefully made ridges, and fertilised with farmyard manure, as well as with commercial fertiliser which everyone referred to as 'bag stuff'. The spade had a sharp cutting edge and was cranked in the middle, while the convenient swing plough was used in the tillage of larger fields. It was a matter of honour that the ridges in the garden should be completed before St. Patrick's Day. When the haulms were about twelve inches high they were sprayed with a mixture of blue stone and water to prevent blight. The crop was harvested in September and if the potatoes were small my father would say disconsolately, 'There's nothin' under them stalks but rosary beads.' The potato picking on the Marshall estate was a big event, with the neighbours coming together in great crowds.

Early summer was the time for cutting the turf. This was still the era of the great turf-cutting *meitheals*, when numbers of men cut and saved each other's turf. The *meitheal* was a hard day's work indeed but the men could be sure of a plentiful supply of food. My mother and grandmother were fond of quoting an old saying which they translated from the Irish; 'Christmas Day and the Day of the Turf— the two days to eat enough.'

The turf in our bog was cut by a *sleán*, while a man with a three-pronged fork tossed the turf to the others on the bank. The man who undertook this task was always strong and vigorous and the technique was known as *brainshing*. The men on the bank then arranged the sods in rows, where they were left to dry before the turf was 'footed' or made into small piles, and then 'stooked' into larger piles. Cutting turf was considered much more than a task in our family. It was an art form which had to be practised correctly or not at all. The sods had to be the right size and depth. They had to be cut smoothly and cleanly, with a dexterity that was a blend of both experience and craftsmanship.

The turf was loaded into a high-railed cart with iron wheels, which was pulled by a donkey from the bog to the side of the road. It was tough work and our little brown donkey was always weary after his efforts at the bog, but he had few working days and could spend much of his time grazing in a field on the Marshall estate. My father loved animals and he never went to the bog without bringing a helping of oats in a bag for the donkey, who would be untackled before settling down to his meal. If the friction of the tackle seemed likely to scar the donkey's back, my father always had old socks and cloths at the ready to protect 'poor old Bill's back'; the cloths were placed under the tackle and thus prevented the formation of any sores. The cart-wheels and the axle were regularly treated with goose grease so that they moved as freely and smoothly as possible.

Every aspect of the bog fascinated me. The textures, and the colours of gold and brown and yellow; the bumble of the bees in purple clumps of heather; the fluffy softness of white bog cotton; the pinkish stones embedded in the turf; the eggs of a nesting curlew or plover; the hardness of bog deal; the insects on the surface of inky waters. It was in these bog-holes that bottles of milk, water and other drinks were kept cold. We children were given the task of lighting the fire and boiling the kettle, which was reserved for trips to the bog and was invariably old and black. While the men sat drinking their tea beside the smoking fire, the older ones always had stories of other turf-cutting days, usually about some local hero who had been 'a great man with a *sleán*'.

After a period of drying in the bog, the turf would be brought home and lovingly created into a rick in the back yard. The sods were clamped or stacked with minute precision; if a sod did not fit properly, it was put aside and another more suitable found. My father or my uncle would take out the fishing boat and cut the river reeds, which were fashioned into sheaves and arranged on top of the rick in a sloping fashion, so that the rain did not lodge on top. When the sheaves were in place, an old fishing net was thrown over them and firmly secured with *gabhlógs*

or Y-shaped sticks which were inserted half way down the rick.

Summer was the time for haymaking, usually July in Callinafercy, though in fine summers it was not unusual to find the sweetly scented meadows ready for cutting in early June. My father still cut hay with the scythe, sharpened by a scythe board or stone. In my childhood summer would not have been summer without the smell of newly mown hay and the meadow would not have been the meadow without the nest of the corncrake. The man with the scythe always left a patch of uncut hay around the corncrake's nest and these uncut sections were familiar sights in most fields of the day. This yellowish-buff-coloured bird with its greyish head and breast was always a joy to see, and we watched with interest as the number of eggs in the nest increased from six to eight to ten. Sometimes there were twelve eggs or more. Then the young brood emerged and the long hot summer nights were alive with the craking of the parent birds as they called to each other through the clover and the daisies.

Hay was turned a number of times with a pitchfork or pike before being made into grasscocks or small cocks. The next stage was the larger cock. These might be taken into a barn but since we did not have one they were made into a single rick which stood in the yard. My uncle Donal was impossible to please when it came to turning hay—there was a right way and a wrong way to turn hay, he said, and I had this uncanny knack of always turning it the wrong way. Likewise when the cocks were being made, he would spend what seemed like hours smoothing it and shaping it, adding a wisp of hay here, removing a 'hampful' there until finally its appearance met with his approval.

Haymaking, like so many other of our outdoor activities, had its moments for fun and relaxation. While the men sat and drank tea and ate apple pie, or took a drink of home-made cider from the earthenware jar, I romped with my sheepdog round the hedgerows, where the fragrance of honeysuckle was heavy on the air and the wild flag iris with its tall yellow flowers and glossy leaves made a dramatic splash of colour. I was always looking for frogs in the grassy margins by the ditch and I loved holding them in my hands, caressing the chilling smoothness of their backs before setting them free once more.

Ripe oats were also cut by the scythe. My father was followed by my mother, who expertly selected sufficient straw for each sheaf. The sheaf was then tied with a piece of twisted straw, and in the evening the field was littered with sheaves of ripened grain. At this stage the sheafs were placed against each other in stooks and each stook was covered with three sheaves turned upside-down to protect the oats from the rain. Before the coming of the thresher, grain was threshed with a flail. Two sticks were carefully chosen, shaped and seasoned, and then hinged together in a time-honoured way. Those who used the flail worked in pairs and struck the rows of sheaves, which were placed on a dry clean floor, in rhythmic alternation. When the first two rows were threshed, the grain was collected and another pair of rows quickly arranged.

One of the greatest delights of my childhood was the day the threshing machine would arrive in the farmyard of the Marshall estate. The puffs of steam had been replaced by the smell of diesel, but nothing could dim the fascination of the machine, as the big black belt whirred round and round, droning with feverish and unerring motion. The cobbled yard was a maelstrom of activity: Men with upturned sleeves tossing sheaves to those on top of the thresher; the owner of the thresher striding about and checking the belt with more than a hint of authority; children running to and fro; the frantic shouts of the men; dogs everywhere; the grain pouring out; above all the rhythmic hum of the machine—a rhythm that was music in our ears.

Meanwhile in the yellow-washed farmhouse, where the great musk rose clambered round the doors, most of its blooms now faded and gone for another year, while hens scratched in the flower garden and the rooks cawed raucously in the treetops, the women of the district were also busy. The tick of the pendulum clock echoed through the whitewashed kitchen as they tended massive pots of potatoes, cabbage and corned beef. When the food was cooked it was arranged on the wide kitchen window, where the two white shutters were drawn back so that sunlight streamed in. Mrs Ruth personally cut the meat, which she transferred from the great blue meat platter on to each separate plate. The men were offered a glass of porter and there was plenty of tea, soda bread, currant bread, brack and apple pie; and beside each plate on the scrubbed wooden table was a single cigarette—a long established custom on threshing day. There was lemonade for the children and rushwork baskets full of apples—which sometimes, in the high-spirited elation of late evening, were hurled about.

The woman usually looked after the poultry. We always had turkeys and hens and new broods were hatched each year. A rusty old tin bath or basin, once used for washing clothes, was filled with hay and served as a nest for the hatching hen. After a week or two, at the slightly ajar door of the darkened shed, my mother would hold each of the eggs in turn towards the light. A dark rim near the top would indicate that the egg was fertile, but none would be discarded until the full hatching period had been completed. There was great satisfaction as the eggs began to crack and the fluffy chicks emerged one by one. The women of the area were always nervous of thundery weather as they believed that thunder killed the tiny birds in the eggs. In the thirties and before, hens, ducks and geese were often put hatching under the dresser, which would have been one of those open types such as Aunt Mag had.

Apart from the hatching season, the eggs were used in home baking and were also sold to the country shops. A brood of goslings was hatched from time to time and my sister delighted in helping the young goslings to emerge from their thick-shelled eggs. 'A gander in the yard is as good as any watchdog,' my mother often said, and indeed the one in our yard was quite aggressive, often stretching his neck and hissing at the inoffensive dog.

As we did not have a turkey cock, during the egg-laying season our turkey had to be taken, on the carrier of the bicycle, to a neighbour of ours, Mrs. Roberts, a journey that took us through the shaded avenue of the Marshall estate where we disturbed the light grey herons that fluttered and squawked overhead. The turkey cock would soon make the acquaintance of our plump white turkey and then we would return home again, removing her from the carrier about half way there so that she could 'stretch her legs'. Because we had little land, the neighbours often allowed our flock of turkeys to wander through the stubble fields when the grain had been cut. Late in the evening, when autumn skies were warm with the afterglow of the sinking sun, I would set off in search of them and herd them slowly home along the winding country road. I hated it when they had to be killed at home but luckily most of them were sold live at the fair in Killorglin.

When the hatching season was upon us much of the talk of my mother and her friends was of hens and eggs. I was quite often sent round the neighbourhood houses in search of a gurry, as we called the hatching hen. One old woman, known for her inclination to gossip, would sometimes stop my mother for a chat on the road, in the middle of which she would suddenly interject, 'Nellie Sullivan, would you be wantin' a hatcher by any chance? She's a fine big hen that would cover a bakers' dozen aisey.' If anyone made a derogatory remark about her tendency to gossip, my mother would speak up in her defence saying, 'Ereh, the craythur, she'd never lave you short of a gurry.'

My mother, however, disliked malicious gossip intensely and often quoted the maxim, 'If you have nothing good to say about a person, say nothing at all.' It was appreciated; on hearing of her death, an old neighbour said, 'Nellie Cronin, is it (Cronin was her maiden name)? She was one quiet woman that never spoke ill of her neighbours.' It was the supreme compliment.

Because the weather was such an all-important factor in our lives, influencing not only sowing and harvesting but the care of animals, our calendar was a rich and colourful patchwork of superstition and saying. If the stars moved quickly across the sky, good weather was at hand, while a golden ring around the moon signified that storms and rain were imminent. Rooks flying low also indicated a storm, and if the mountains seemed closer than usual rain was on the way. A robin hopping near the door indicated frost, while the sound of a cat purring was taken as a sign of dry, hard, windy weather. One heron implied rain but if two herons were seen this meant good weather.

Every month of the year had its own particular saws of wisdom. The first three days of April were usually cold and were known as the borrowed days, the days that April borrowed from March, while every beekeeper knew that:

> A swarm of bees in May is worth a load of hay;
> A swarm of bees in June is worth a silver spoon;
> A swarm of bees in July isn't worth a fly.

Mornings and evenings were times of particular import:

> A rainbow at night is the shepherd's delight;
> A rainbow in the morning is the shepherd's warning,

while another version forecast:

> Evenings red and mornings grey,
> Set the traveller on his way.
> Evenings grey and mornings red,
> Pour down rain on the traveller's head.

Many of the best-known sayings had their origins in farming forecasts:

> An ounce of March dust is worth a king's ransom;
> A wet and windy May fills the barn with corn and hay;
> A wet May and a dry June makes the farmer whistle
>   a tune;
> A shower in July is worth a plough of oxen;
> Never trust a July sky;
> A dry summer never begs bread.

4
The Salt Sea Air

My father, one of a family of eleven, two of whom died at an early age, was born in a little two-roomed cottage on the very edge of the River Laune, which had once been used as a bathing house by members of the Godfrey family. My great-great-grandmother had been laundry woman to the Godfreys for many years and family tradition is that when they decided to abandon it, they presented it to her in appreciation of long years of devoted service. There was only a small boundary wall between it and the river and the foaming waves of swirling spray lashed against the wall of the house on dark winter nights. My father often told us about the nights when the children of the house huddled together, listening to the howl of the wind and watching the spray cascading down the tiny panes of glass in the window. The little house, because of its location, was a favourite meeting-place for the fishermen of the area who referred to it affectionately as 'the palace'.

A travel writer noted in 1845 that Killorglin was a fishing village on the River Laune, 'where the inhabitants cure an immense quantity of fish for the London market'. The kingdom of wave and wind was a powerful influence on our lives and many of the families in the neighbourhood, like that of my father, had been fishermen for generation after generation.

In the early years of the century the local fishermen fished for herring as well as for salmon. My neighbour Jackie Harmon sometimes told me about the days of the herring fishing in the thirties and before:

The men from the Cliff and Callinafercy used to go herring fishing years ago. They fished for herring back near Cromane, at a place called the Towers. It was called that because old castles and towers were often seen beneath the water when the tide was calm and blue. They generally fished for herring by night, especially moonlit nights, because that was thought to be the best time. They used to take with them an old black pot with a piece of turf lighting in it. They used this fire to light their pipes and fags because they seldom had matches in those days. The women often walked as far as Castlemaine with a *cliabh* of herrings on their backs, where they tried to sell them to make a few shillings.

Another story underlines the importance of the herring season in those days:

When one of the lads, a fisherman, was working in North Kerry, he told his wife to send him a telegram when she got word that the herring shoals had come to Cromane. 'Twas dear to send a wire and people had little money. So she conveyed the message in three words: 'Tim. Herring in.'

The offices of the KRD fisheries in Killorglin had been exporting salmon from the area for decades. Much of it ended up on high society tables in the elegant dining-rooms of socialite London, and Laune salmon acquired a fine reputation in the world of international cuisine. There was a plentiful supply of fish on the river in those days which the fishermen of the area exploited to the full, but always with unspoken respect for the power of the sea and the laws of the wild.

The distinctive wing-beat of swans flying south was taken as a sign that winter was over and spring was at hand. Then all was activity, preparing the nets and boats for the new season. A great deal of skill and craftsmanship was involved. Nets were carefully examined and holes or tears repaired. I can still vividly recall my father and the local fishermen standing on the strand mending their nets. With what dexterity they moved the fishing needle in and out through the meshes! With what precision they gauged the various distances, using not a ruler but a stick known as a *caighdean* that had previously been measured; the length varied according to the size of the mesh.

Oars were mended by encircling the damaged area with a band or hoop of steel. Augers, the short lengths of timber nailed on to the top or gunnel of the boat, into which were inserted two delphins—narrow rounded lengths of timber, pointed at the end and used to hold the oar in position while the stroke was being taken—also needed occasional replacing. The augur was affixed at the point where the oar passed out across the boat and thus it served to strengthen and protect the gunnel from any chafing and friction. Two further pieces of timber, called clamps, were attached to the oar to prevent it from coming into contact with the augur, since friction of any kind would wear away both augur and oar.

The final stage was the tarring of the boats. The tar was boiled on the strand in old containers or tins and applied when cool to the upturned boat. The top section was then painted, to 'add a touch of colour' my father said. Our boat was stored in a shed which had a roof that had been thatched by my uncle using reeds and willow spars. During late spring and early summer, it provided a home for twittering swallows and other nesting birds. At first they were nervous of the presence of children but soon they grew more familiar and flitted in and out, almost totally oblivious of us.

The making of boats and nets had always been carried on in the neighbourhood. Annie Sullivan, who owned the beautiful thatched cottage near us, had been the local net-maker in the early years of the century. The fishermen of the Cliff and Callinafercy and even further afield—from Cromane, Gurrane and Scrahan—brought her 'pounds' or reels of cotton hemp. The hemp was wound round an implement called the winding blades which stood in the centre of the floor. Annie's niece, Eileen Murphy, recalled Annie seated at the table, moving the fishing needles with skill and rapidity as she made the nets. These nets were generally made in the springtime, and Annie had learned the art from her father who had also been a net-maker. The net consisted of three basic parts. The section of net which was first cast out from the boat was called the *sciathán*. Then came 'the bunt' or central section where the fish were ensnared, and finally the wing which was the last cast out but the first drawn in when the haul was being made. The boatbuilder at that time was Tom Naughton who was based at the fishery office in Killorglin.

From February to the end of July the talk in our house was constantly about fish and fishing. About low tide and high tide and the flood in the river. About Jer's boat and Thady's boat—in fact, every boat on the Maine. There were at least six fishing boats in the area in those days and lots had to be drawn to decide who should fish which pools and on which days. All the local fishing pools had Irish names, such as *Poll Dubh*, *Poll-a-Curran*, *Cos Caol* and *Lurga*. Fishing ceased in Lurga in the fifties because a massive tree stump, embedded in the seabed, continually tore the nets. My father often said, 'But for that *acaran* in Lurga, there'd be great fishing there,'—*acaran* being a word for obstruction.

It was believed that the first haul of the day would be better than all the rest, for 'the first crew would have the sweepin' of the pool', and sometimes if there were a few boats at the pier at the Store, they had a race back to the Banks or over to Poll-a-Curran to see which boat would get the first haul. Though very often it didn't prove to be nearly as bountiful as anticipated, faith in it remained unshaken. When one of the fishermen went to town one day, he met a friend. 'He asked me did we get the first haul,' he explained later. 'Not wan word about did we get any fish, lads, for he thinks the first haul is an honour in itself.' However, such races were seen as good practice for the regatta, and if sometimes an oar got broken, there was always a spare one in the bottom of the boat.

Lots were also drawn to decide who should keep the first trout of the season which was regarded as a special prize. My mother, being methodical, always kept records of various catches in a little red book, and those old records show that catches of sixty to seventy salmon were not uncommon on good days. It was a tradition that each fisherman should get one salmon free during the season; this my mother cooked in the big black pot over the fire, and it tasted delicious with potatoes and cabbage or lettuce. Occasionally we had flounder or fluke as we called them, but we simply couldn't stomach mullet because the taste was so strong. Once or twice my mother cooked the mullet and dished them out to the hens but my father said that the eggs tasted of mullet for weeks afterwards. Our neighbour Mary, however, thought mullet were 'only grand fish altogether', so she was more than welcome to any we had.

The fishermen of my youth worked hard, often in dangerous conditions, but their sense of humour never deserted them. Once when they were fishing the Maine, they were getting no salmon. Some of the crew wondered if the salmon had deserted the river, whereupon one wag on board remarked, 'Sure, if I was a salmon myself, 'tisn't up the Maine I'd come.' Another time, when the mud at the river's edge was very sticky, it was recommended to the self-same gentleman that he should walk a little more lightly. 'How can I walk a bit lighter?' he wondered. 'For amn't I still the same weight I was ten seconds ago.'

When I was at school it was still the practice to take the fish to the KRD offices in Killorglin by donkey and cart, though the fishing itself had been transferred to the River Maine. After school I would rush home and hastily tackle the donkey. Then my mother and I would sit on bags of straw in the cart and make the long long journey along the grey winding roads to the river banks. It was pleasant on warm summer days, when the songs of birds cascaded

through the trees and the marshy fields shone bright with
the beauty of the yellow flag iris. When it rained, however,
the grey coil of road seemed to meander endlessly before
us.

When we reached the river I would often clamber across
the drain to the bank, to see the men making a haul, the
salmon splashing in the water like living silver in the
afternoon sun. When we had taken our precious cargo on
board we travelled off towards the office where the fish
were weighed, their bodies gleaming against the darkness
of the scales. Sometimes they were placed in the ice-house
for storage; sometimes they were instantly packed and
covered with broken ice. Then there was the slow plodding
road home, the little brown donkey growing more and more
weary with each passing second. It was usually half-past
eight in the evening when we arrived back in the yard where
hungry turkeys and hens were waiting. The donkey had
to be untackled and they all had to be fed before we could
think of ourselves.

I kept a diary intermittently at the time and one entry
sums up the summer holidays routine: 'Cycled to town with
fish in the morning. I was not long home when I had to
tackle the donkey to go to Cul Inch for more fish. Mom
went with me. It's very tiring—and we have to make this
long journey at least three times a week. And it's nothing
but gobble, gobble, gobble by the turkeys when we get
home.'

When fish had to be stored overnight, we wrapped them
in damp cloths as we had no way of getting ice. Occasionally
our cat managed to swipe a tail or a head, and the guilty
creature would be in my father's 'black book' for the next
few days.

There were many superstitions about the choice of day on
which the fishing season should begin. Friday was considered
particularly propitious, while Monday was regarded with

more than a little distrust. Sometimes the boat might be taken from the little thatched shed on Monday evening and rowed by oar to the fishing grounds, but no fishing would be undertaken until the early hours of Tuesday morning. 'You'd have no luck if you started fishing of a Monday,' my uncle said. No one ever went fishing herring on a Saturday night, because if they did, according to a strong local tradition, the sea would rise and rear like a wild horse and the boats would be forced to seek the shelter of the cove from the howling wind and the raging swell. A similar fate awaited those who dared to venture on the waves on Good Friday:

> *Níor chuaigh bád mór chun farraige Aoine an Chéasta chun uallach gainnimh a thabhairt abhaile léi. Tugadh gála mór uirthi aon turas a rachadh sí ann agus beígean di chur isteach sa chuan ón gála.* (No boat ever went to sea to collect a load of sand on Good Friday. A great storm would develop if it did so, and would force it to seek shelter in the cove.)

In the fifties, a high tide presaged bad weather, while the movements of sea birds and wild ducks also provided an indication of weather prospects. When seagulls flew low or moved far inland, bad weather was on the way; my father never liked to see them 'ould *faoileáins*' around the place. Wild ducks in the fields were likewise unwelcome, but lapwings or *pilibíns* in great flocks received a less hostile reception, since their arrival made little or no difference to weather prospects.

But we didn't depend solely on weather signs; we took additional precautions. No crew ventured on the waves without having a bottle of holy water somewhere on board and my father insisted that our boat should be blessed by one of the local priests at the spring stations each year. Some of the fishermen not only blessed the nets; they also thought it prudent to hang a holy medal from one of the meshes. Nevertheless, on stormy nights there were many anxious moments for my mother as she waited for the fishermen to return safely. What a sense of relief came upon her when she saw the flash-lights on the bicycles glimmering faintly through the wind-whipped darkness of the night.

Fishing, being an unpredictable business at the best of times, was subject to the vagaries of luck. We were all well versed in the various omens, which could, it was thought, be helped along by prayer. Alas, the efficacy of prayer was sometimes in doubt. Bob Knightly told me the following sad story:

> There were four boats on the Maine in the old days—Jimín's, Danín's, The Captain's (the local nickname for Dan Linehan's father) and Thade Kenny's. Wan of the fishermen, Pat M—, was a rough kind of man. Wan morning when the men were goin' fishing at the banks he found that the rest had gone off before him. When Pat came to the banks he found the men down on their knees in their boats saying the rosary. Well he cursed um, tellin' um they should be out hauling long before that. The wans that did all the prayin' didn't get wan salmon, and Pat M— got eight or nine.

No doubt the unlucky 'wans' transferred their trust to more traditional omens.

The buzz of the bumble-bee or the lazy purr of a contented cat were music in the fishermen's ears, since they both implied good luck. If a new moon appeared while the boat was out fishing, each member of the crew had to remove a coin from his pocket and examine the upturned side; a majority of heads was taken as a sign of good luck. This tradition, as well as another which suggested that it was lucky for the fishermen to spit into the mouth of the first fish caught, had lapsed in the fifties. Another old belief was that if half a fish was eaten and the remainder returned to the water, the subsequent year the whole fish would return to the very same place and wait to be caught. The view that the sale of any fish to a person with broad thumbs should be frowned upon had also faded from memory in my childhood days.

All the fishermen of the older generation considered it very unlucky to meet a red-haired girl or woman as they went on their way to fish. Indeed some of them went so far as to return home on such occasions, implicitly believing that their efforts would be totally in vain for the rest of the day. Girls like my sister were, thus, never a welcome sight to fishermen about to set out in their boats.

One of the most colourful fishing beliefs amongst the older generation in Callinafercy concerned the hour when the fish fell asleep:

> The fish will sleep from twelve till wan. 'Tis the dead hour of night and if you were out in the trap you'd hear nothing but the axle. After wan, you'd hear the chirpin' of the birds and the croakin' of the frogs. That time, the croakin' of the frogs from the bogs kept people awake all night. You could never catch the fish during that hour, for they were sound asleep somewhere. Jimín it was that told me that story and he knew 'twas true for he never caught um during that hour though he tried often.

James Clifford of the Store told me that one of the older fishermen, Thade Kenny, had a great fund of stories about fairies and ghosts. Thade insisted that he regularly met the celebrated black dog of Callinafercy on his way back from the pier, a path which was known locally as *Cul Tragh* (literally, the back strand). According to local tradition, Lurga was the most haunted spot on the River Maine, so in the days before the embedded tree stump ended fishing there, boats were very loath to fish there singly at night.

Fish, particularly the salmon, figured prominently in folk stories. One related how St. Patrick asked a group of fishermen for a salmon. They promised him the first one caught, but when they caught one they moved out into the bay and jeered the saint from afar. Under the water a plaice began to laugh with derision, whereupon St. Patrick said to it, 'May your mouth always stay as it is now.' This curse explains why the plaice has a crooked mouth. Next moment a great salmon leaped out of the water, silver scales flashing in the sunlight, into Patrick's hands, offering himself to the saint. St. Patrick blessed the salmon and that is why it has the highest leap of any fish in the river.

Fishermen in Callinafercy were sometimes troubled by seals and otters. It was believed that the otter would hold

on to one's leg (if he managed to grab hold of it) until he heard the bone crack—a belief that was also held about badgers in several parts of Kerry. Here is a local story about the seal:

Wan time the fishermen of the Cliff were plagued by a seal playing on their nets. He was clayning (cleaning) um out. They asked Sergeant Fay in Killorglin to come down and shoot the seal. Ned Guinah (McKenna) was a great singer and he started singing *The Rangers of the Laune* as they were going down in the boat. The Laune Rangers football team in Killorglin were after winning a big match and they were after makin' up a song about it:

> They were kicking up the leather
> While the points were scoring down,
> And many a shout was heard that day,
> For the Rangers of the Laune

The old people were great for making songs. Old Micháel (Thade's father) could make a song while you'd be lookin' at him. Well, Sergeant Fay shot the seal in the end.

It was true that the old people were always 'making' songs and many had references to fishing. One of my favourites was *The Hills of Kilderry*:

Away down in Kilderry, where oft in my childhood,
I roamed through your woods with a heart free from care,
And gathered the fruits from the vines in the wild woods,
And plucked the wild roses perfuming the air.
And often at evening when homeward returning,
I watched the sun setting beyond the blue vale.
And, oh with what joy my young heart was burning,
As I hoped in Kilderry I would always remain.

How delightful to walk through the fields of Kilderry,
When the sun in the west sheds its rays o'er the scene,
And the boatmen of Lurga are crossing the ferry,
And casting their nets in the rushy Tureen.
That serpentine river with its silvery waters,
Moves calm and serene through valley and swamp;
Further off in the twilight the far distant mountain,
Could be seen from Kilderry on the high road to Camp.

Most rivers in Kerry had some association with a mermaid,

and the Laune was no exception. This story was told in the thirties:

> Hundreds of years ago, pearls were seen along the strand of the River Laune. Every evening about sunset, a lovely young girl used to be seen picking them. It seems that she was not a real girl at all. She was half a girl and half a salmon. She was called a mermaid. One day an old woman was sitting on a stone near the river when she saw the beautiful maiden splashing among the waves with her tail. The foolish old woman put her hand into the water, trying to catch her, but the mermaid pulled her in and she was drowned. That night three or four men went looking for the old woman. The mermaid saw them coming and she began to sing, but they struck her with their oars and killed her. She was never seen again.

As children in the fifties we were often told stories of the strange but magnificent sea creatures, the porpoises, which came to the local cove just a decade before. They were, said one man, with the understatement of the born story-teller, as big as horses and were snorting heavily as they passed up the Laune by the side of the Cliff. The noise frightened some people when they heard it at first because the majority of locals had never seen a porpoise before.

5
The Country House

On those beautiful long evenings of a Kerry June, soft with the blues and greens of mountain and lake, when everywhere was alive with colour—the creamy white flowers of the elder, golden honeysuckle, old pink roses and yellow flag irises— we would pause, if passing through Milltown, to admire the magnificent rhododendron which grew at the entrance gates to Kilcoleman Abbey, home of the Godfrey family and largest of the three great houses in our neighbourhood. Nobody knew when it had been planted but it had been part of the Milltown scene for as long as anyone remembered.

It was traditionally believed that the Godfreys, who by now had become baronets and High Sheriffs of Kerry, built their stately home in 1772—a plaque on a wall bore that date—but recent research indicates that it was probably a reconstruction of an earlier tower-house. Originally called Milltown House, it was set in a wooded demesne, with superb orchards and walled gardens. The architect, William Vitruvius Morrison, who specialised in Greek and Tudor-Revival styles, drew up elaborate plans for an extensive remodelling of the house in 1819, but these plans were only partially implemented, two decades later, in the 1830s. Nevertheless Kilcoleman Abbey, as the Godfrey home was now called, was an impressive building and it dominated the Milltown skyline for almost a hundred and fifty years. One of the four corner turrets was said to be the armoury of the Godfreys, who were involved with the Kerry Militia and local yeomanry groups such as the Milltown Fusiliers; a harp and crown appeared side by side, below a sprig of shamrock, on a medal of the latter brigade. We were told that it was raided during the War of Independence in 1921 and a cache of arms was taken by the insurgents.

Kilcoleman did not have a gate lodge, though a period house close to the massive entrance gates served that purpose in the waning years of the estate. The gates, flanked by two imposing pillars of stone, and the long perimeter wall represented, as did all the great houses of Ireland, the wealth and the status of the Ascendancy.

In the late fifties, the family, represented by Miss Phyllis Godfrey, still lived in Kilcoleman, and though the exterior was beginning to crumble we children marvelled at its grace and elegance. Alas, it has since been demolished and the splendid rhododendron has likewise vanished.

Naturally the doings of the Godfreys, past and present, were much discussed by the local families and many were the stories told about them. My favourite was about the haunted room at the Abbey, rather appropriately numbered thirteen. The door of this room was kept securely locked at all times and no one was ever allowed to sleep in it. Strangers to the house invariably reported that they had heard strange unearthly sounds coming from the forbidden room at the witching hour of midnight. When the last Sir John Godfrey attempted to install central heating in the house, sometime during the thirties, a firm of plumbers from Lismore in County Waterford was engaged to do the work. The men, who were billeted in one of the rooms beside number thirteen, were forced to evacuate it after two nights, driven out by strange sounds which they described as being like the voices of monks, zealously chanting their holy office. They were unaware of the ruins of the Abbey of Killagha in the neighbourhood or of the fact that the Godfreys had been granted the Abbey lands.

The drawing-room also had its ghost—an ethereal lady who played the piano. One pleasant summer evening as a gardener walked past the drawing-room window he peered inside and saw a gracious lady, dressed in period costume, seated at the piano. Drifting through the windows into the fragrant gardens beyond was music which was so sweet and celestial that he could hardly tear himself away. When he later enquired who the lady visitor was, he was told that there was no one staying in the house at the time.

No great family would be complete without its eccentrics and the Godfreys were no exception. One of them, following a disagreement with other members of the family, proceeded to bury all his gold, coins, jewels and precious family heirlooms in a field not far from the family home—firmly identified by many of my father's generation as one adjoining the nearby Abbey of Killagha. When he had buried the treasure, this volatile Godfrey joined the Kerry Militia and rushed off to serve in some foreign campaign. Nothing was ever heard of him again and it was presumed that he had been killed in action. In the late fifties a local man unearthed a black metal box in one of the fields around the Abbey. Naturally, having heard the story of the buried treasure many a time, he felt sure he had the Godfrey gold within his grasp. Much to his disappointment, however, he found only a gilded regimental badge bearing the number 36 and surmounted by the royal crest. It was also inscribed with the Garter motto: *Honi soit qui mal y pense*.

A Sir John Godfrey of the nineteenth century, reproached with his habit of getting up at lunch-time, is reported to have replied, 'The fact is, I sleep very slow.'

The Godfreys were prominent on the social scene in the Kerry of the late nineteenth century, when hunting, shooting and fishing were the regulation pursuits of the country gentry. The Godfrey Hounds are thought to have originally been called the 'Milltown Chace'. Sir John Fermor Godfrey, 1828-1900, compiled a number of hunting diaries, some of which survive. Several names of horses are listed—simple endearing names such as Billy, Katey, and Dan. There are several references, too, to the buying and selling of horses. The entry for 11 August, 1876, reads: 'Puck Fair: Bought Bay mare, 5-year-old, by Beautiful Star. Broke the record on price of colt.' In another entry (1877) Sir John mentions that he was trying to buy a pair of horses for Maurice O'Connell, son of the Liberator. The diary mainly consists of very concise descriptions of the hunt. '8 Jan, 1878: Own hounds at Rockfield Bridge. Field 35. Sport AI. Foxhunt for 9 miles. Eleven people down—two ladies and also self.'

Local reporters were somewhat more expansive:

Those hounds kept by that thorough sportsman, Sir John Godfrey, met at Rockfield Bridge. The morning was fine but the muster to meet Mangan the huntsman was rather small. A hare was soon found, but after a short run the scent failed. Trotted back again and found another hare immediately. Quarry ran across Rockfield Hill, through Kearney's farm, and then faced for Kultis Hill, after which she ran by Batterfield House and the village of Firies. Finally, a severe hail shower coming on, she was lost not far from Farranfore station. The distance covered in this run was at least seven miles, with only two trifling checks throughout, while the line of country being taken was nearly all grass, the going was fast and furious. Mr John Coltsman on his favourite hunter, The Gander, and Mr James O'Connor were conspicuous in the front rank from start to finish.

The country people of Milltown were not over-impressed by the antics of the hunt. Mrs. Teahan from Milltown told us a story she had heard from her grandmother:

My grandmother used make her apron out of a meal bag—a bag that had held meal at one time. She used to bring turf into the fire in the apron and inside in the turf one day, didn't she find a little hare and he almost lifeless after being chased by the Godfreys and their hounds. 'Did he stay there?' says I to her. 'Ereh no, a chroí,' says she. 'He struggled away as best he could.' She added, as a footnote, 'When the hunt was on, you know, the riders didn't care about trampling on stalks and crops and knocking fences all over the place.'

The Godfreys owned a decorative hunting-lodge on the Killorglin road, which was the scene of many lively picnics, parties and night-time revelries, which continued well into the twentieth century. A neighbour, Jackie Harmon, told us, 'It was said by my father that blood and hair were mixed with the mortar on the walls of the lodge and that the mortar would never crumble because of that.' The walls, however, have now crumbled and collapsed into a state of decay.

On the whole, the Godfreys were fairly well regarded, and there are vague folk memories about their generosity during the famine. One recollection: 'I heard a story that the Godfrey's steward was ordered to kill five cows for the starving people.' Sir William Godfrey was also remembered for giving timber for fuel to poorer households.

If the glories of Kilcoleman Abbey were beginning to fade in the fifties, the large country house of the Marshalls at Callinafercy, just a few hundred yards from our cottage, was still very much as it had always been. The house had been built in 1861 by Richard John Leeson-Marshall, great-grandson of the first Earl of Milltown. In her book, *The Winds of Time*, Lady Edith Gordon noted that despite the proximity of a beautiful bay, the house was badly sited and commanded scarcely any view of the mountains. This, of course, was only a personal opinion, and it must be said that the house has a great deal of architectural merit.

Richard John Leeson-Marshall married Rebecca Power, daughter of the Venerable Archdeacon Power of Lismore. His son, Markham Leeson-Marshall, was educated at New College, Oxford, graduated to the post of Major in the Royal Munster Fusiliers, 3rd Battalion, and became High Sheriff of Kerry in 1890. He was also a Justice of the Peace. He married Mabel Godfrey, who died when her baby (the Mrs. Ruth of my childhood) was just a few months old. Major Marshall married again in 1906, this time to Meriel Hodson, daughter of Sir George Hodson.

The Leeson-Marshalls also owned a hunting-lodge in the valley of Claodach or Clydagh, not far from the borders of Cork and Kerry. It was here that my mother was born, in an old farmhouse beside a mountain stream, with a view of the majestic Da Chich Danann or the Paps always in the distance. According to family tradition, her great-grandfather was the first Cronin to come and live in the valley of Claodach. He had apparently been evicted from his holding in the Macroom area in County Cork, and had only been allowed to take a horse with him. His name was Prionsias Ó Crónin and he lived to the ripe old age of 105, dying in the early nineteenth century. The life of one of his sons, Tadgh Prionsias, spanned almost another century, from 1823 to 1914. His son Patrick, who was born in 1862, was my grandfather. As a child my mother, who was called 'little Ellie' because her mother's name was also Ellen, grew up in a family that spoke fluent Irish—the rosary was recited in Irish every night. When her aunt Margaret died at the

age of nineteen, it proved a tragic inspiration for her uncle
Frank. He wrote this poem in her memory in April 1892:

> Oh little sister, sister dear,
>   This is a world of pain.
> I know my words thou wilt not hear,
>   But we will meet again.
> Meanwhile 'twill soothe a brother's grief,
>   To pen a doleful lay,
> That sorrow may find some relief,
>   This lonely lonely day.
>
> And oh, 'tis sad to think, to know,
>   Thy face no more I'll see.
> And that each year will come and go,
>   And bring no word from thee.
> But there's a land beyond the grave,
>   Where angels ever shine.
> Where sorrow dare not waft his wave,
>   That land I know is thine.
>
> The day without is bright and clear—
>   'Tis sad within this room.
> So sad that I could with thee share,
>   The silence of the tomb.
> Thou wilt not heed a brother's tears,
>   Upon thy bosom shed.
> But thou wilt go and sleep for years,
>   Within thy lonely bed.
>
> And thou wilt go to slumber there,
>   Before the sun has set.
> Oh, what a lonely sleeping place—
>   So cold, so damp, so wet.
> His Will be done for He doth know,
>   What for us each is best.
> And who would linger here below,
>   When called by Him to rest.

Grand-uncle Frank became a regional Head Constable in the Royal Irish Constabulary; he died at the barracks in Carrick-on-Suir in 1919.

My uncle Frank also wrote many songs and poems in Irish and English, and won prizes for the beauty of his lyrics. One of my favourites in Irish is entitled *An Ait ud Claodach in ar Rugadh Me*, which loosely translated means *Claodach; Where I was Born*. The poem describes the great mountains standing guard over the valley of Claodach, the sunlight causing the furze to blaze more brightly still, little rivulets making music beside the hillocks and birds singing sweetly in every bush, sometimes with variations in their songs as if they were trying out new compositions of their own— which I have always thought to be a charming notion. The last lines refer to the River Flesk, 'going home' to Loch Lein in Killarney:

Ós my chóir na seasamh bhi radharc gan easnamh,
An Dá Chích Danainn go hard sa spéir.
Is cnocaí árda go tréan moráldha
Ag déanamh garda don gleann go léir.
An grian ag taitneam ghun fraoch dá lasa,
Os carraigeacha tré ceannabhán.
Ar glaisí glórmhaire, ar sruthán beomhaire,
Is caisí ceolmhaire faoi gach cnochán.

Do bhí cantain einin ar sceach is geagín,
A poirtín féinig as uile bhéil,
As ard a scórnaigh bhí loinn is smólaigh,
Ag traill na nótai a chum siad féin.
Ba bhinn an ceol sin a bhi gá seoladh,
Amach as beola píop is píoban,
Is i lár a ghleanna abha mór na Fleasga,
Ag dul abahile go Locha Léin.

When my mother was seventeen, in 1929, she met Mrs. Marshall who was on one of her hunting trips to the valley, and that was how she came to Callinafercy. Domestic service was one of the few jobs open to girls at that time, and my mother's sister worked at the magnificent house built by the Herberts at Muckross, Killarney. The house was then owned by the Vincents, a wealthy American family, who 'entertained royally and gardened imperially'.

Mrs Marshall was tall and stately in appearance, with delicate gold-rimmed glasses. During the day she wore finely tailored costumes—jackets and skirts—the hemline of the skirt falling midway between knee and foot. She spent much of her time in the gardens, where she was assisted by a head-gardener, an under-gardener and an assistant. My paternal grandfather (who was known locally as John D.) had in fact been involved in the initial development of the gardens, when great quantities of earth had to be carted about to create the sloping flower banks and split-level lawns. Local tradition has it that part of the payment for the workmen in those early days was a barrel of porter every day, which may account for the saying that 'porter makes the flowers grow in Callinafercy'! My grandfather was also credited with building the finely crafted stone walls round the estate, particularly round the garden.

According to my mother, Mrs. Marshall was generally very friendly, but she could also be strict at times. It was the rule of the house that servants should be in their bedrooms before eleven o'clock at night. My mother remembered returning late one summer's night, when she had been for a stroll with my father (whom she was courting at the time), to find Mrs. Marshall waiting for her in the kitchen. There followed a lengthy tirade on the theme that rules were rules and had to be observed.

Patience was not one of her virtues. When my mother was assistant-cook in the early thirties, the cook, Kathleen, would generally take an hour's rest in the afternoon. Mrs. Marshall would sometimes become impatient and knock at the bedroom door, asking politely, 'Are you resting, Kathleen?' to which came the inevitable reply, 'Yes, Mrs.

Marshall, I'm resting.' The lady of the house would then withdraw gracefully, only to return some moments later with the same question, this time with a little more emphasis, 'Are you *still* resting, Kathleen?' With equal emphasis would come the reply, 'Yes, Mrs. Marshall, I'm *still* resting.'

Hygiene was high on her list of priorities. When a servant returned from Killorglin with groceries and came to her with the change, she would refuse to take any coins in her hand without first donning a glove. Country dirt was tolerable, she said, but one could so easily get disease from dirty coins; one simply did not know who might have handled them before. She was also slightly eccentric when it came to drinking her tea; even though she normally used her right hand, she drank her tea from a cup held in her left hand—a practice that could be relied on to rescue the conversation among the guests when they had exhausted all other topics.

Her husband, known locally as the Major, had been in the British army. During the day he generally wore a jacket and waistcoat over knickerbockers laced at the knee and knee-length socks. He smoked a finely curved pipe, and carried an amber-coloured cane with a shepherd's crook effect at the top. He was very fond of fishing and shooting and the estate had its own resident gamekeeper until 1940. In addition to his pipe, the Major also smoked Craven A cigarettes, which came in attractive little tin boxes. Whenever he visited the national school in the thirties, he would distribute a collection of them amongst the children in various classes. One old man recalled that 'those precious tin boxes were treated like gold by the children'.

At one time, he had been the local Resident Magistrate, travelling in a pony and trap to the old Courthouse at Bridge Street, Milltown, every Wednesday during the law term. Then he would proceed up the impressive stone staircase at the back of the building to the court rooms on the first floor, there to preside over the local Petty Sessions. The offences were usually minor, though a few hardened regulars appeared before him again and again on charges of drunk and disorderly behaviour. When these local celebrities made their appearance in the dock, they invariably attracted a crowd to the courthouse and they were usually rewarded by some quick-witted exchanges between the magistrate and the accused. In general, the Major was considered to be a rather lenient RM.

The Marshalls, like nearly all their class in those days, were loyal to the British crown. In the years prior to 1922 songs in praise of the reigning British monarch were a regular feature of any children's parties they gave, and the country children were constantly reminded of the blessings bestowed upon Ireland by the royal family across the Irish sea. Mugs which featured an engraved portrait of the monarch were often given to the children as a gift. One old man still has in his possession a mug from one of the Callinafercy Christmas parties, once a child's plaything, now a treasured memento of the past, and not without value as an antique.

Children's parties were part of the way of life at Callinafercy. One of the highlights of the year was the annual school party, which was held in the fort field overlooking Dingle Bay. A contemporary hand-written account of one such party reads:

About three o'clock, two hundred juveniles from all directions in the neighbourhood assembled at the park in Callinafercy. Several races were improvised between the youngsters, but the events that created the most interest were the obstacle race and the tug-of-war. In the former, fifteen lads were sent off from the starting-point. First they had to negotiate a low stone wall, over which several came to grief; next they had to get through the rungs of a ladder laid down on its side, and finally to creep under a large sail, entering at one end and coming out at the opposite.

Meanwhile in the tug-of-war there were twelve contestants on each team—all of them about twelve years old—and there was apparently 'much merriment' amongst the spectators when the first rope snapped, spilling both teams backwards on to the field. A new rope was soon procured and the better team won after a hard struggle.

Lady Gordon distributed the prizes to the pupils who had obtained the best marks at the last results examination, the names being taken from the examination roll. In cases where several pupils of the same class obtained equal marks, all were awarded prizes. Several prizes were presented for needlework and the ladies expressed much pleasure at the excellence of the specimens exhibited.

Lady Gordon was deputising for her brother (Major Marshall), who was away with his regiment, and she donated two special prizes of her own for the best attenders at the school, for—to quote the account—'good attendance is the secret of success'.

These parties were not only for the children; the entire population of the locality attended, 'old folks and children making the day a general holiday'.

It is perhaps hard for people today to appreciate the importance of the country house to its immediate neighbourhood in those days. The Leeson-Marshalls were not just the owners of Callinafercy. They were the setters of standards, the arbitrators of taste, the landlords, employers, benefactors, law-enforcers, and often the only refuge of the poor and needy. As children we were often told the story of a poor family in the twenties, who lived about seven miles away. The father of the family died and the children came to Mrs. Marshall pleading for help. She promptly provided them with blankets and other supplies and one of the most vivid memories of the older generation was the sight of those children struggling home along the sea-shore, their backs bowed down with the provisions they had been given by the lady of the big house.

Life at Callinafercy revolved around the family's circle of friends and a set pattern of life dictated by the time of the day and the season of the year. Life moved at the leisurely pace that wealth and connections made possible. Remote from the cares of the kitchen, Mrs. Marshall played the piano before dinner and spent a great deal of her time arranging the flowers for the drawing-room. It was a self-contained little world with almost everything that was needed being produced locally on the estate, an ordered society in which everyone knew his or her place; there would always be horses in the stables and servants below stairs. And that, of course, was the key to this pleasant way of life. It was only possible because of the largely unseen army of people who worked in and around the big house. And if these people sometimes wished for a different and freer pattern to *their* lives, at least they had the security of a job, usually a roof over their heads and regular meals.

Entertainment at Callinafercy was constant and lavish. Friends were invited to luncheon and dinner or they might call for afternoon tea, served outdoors if the weather was fine or in the drawing-room. Tea parties were also held in the doll's house, a small fairy-tale cottage set deep in the heart of the woods, which had been built for the daughter of the house. Beneath an enchanting moss-green roof, which was trimmed with elaborately carved woodwork, a heavy green gothic doorway led into the single room. A little glass cabinet with latticed green doors, built into one of the interior walls, also had panels of fine plasterwork and held an array of miniature tea-cups, just waiting to be placed on the table, and a selection of toys for the amusement of the guests. Two tiny windows looked out across a winding woodland path—a path that Red Riding Hood might well have travelled on her way to her Granny's. Grown-ups, apart from the servants, might be invited to these tea-parties but this was at the discretion of the hostess. Nearby, an ornamental pond full of placid water, reflected the sunlight that filtered through the tall trees, just one of the many decorative stone ponds which were part of the original plan of the estate.

Tennis parties were held on the higher lawn, which was reached by stone steps with highly ornate urns on either side. The maids, in their blue and white uniforms, carried out trays of drinks between games, and as they relaxed the players could admire the gardens or study the gargoyled faces which jutted out from the wall above the windows of the house. A stroll might take them down the gravel walkway leading to the back avenue under a canopy of trees.

Autumn and winter were the seasons for shooting in the woods around. Pheasant and woodcock were specially reared for these shooting parties, which always meant intensive preparation in advance. Wire barriers had to be erected here and there among the trees, and local men were hired as beaters to advance through the undergrowth with sticks, to encourage the game birds to rise skywards when they met a barrier. Once a year the Marshall household travelled to their lodge on the purple hills of Claodach, where there was an abundant supply of pheasant and grouse. My mother often travelled to the lodge with the family, which was something of a holiday for her as the house had its own staff and she could take time off for a short visit to her old home.

The guests of the Leeson-Marshalls came mainly from the countryside around, the most frequent being Sir William and Lady Mary Godfrey from nearby Kilcoleman Abbey. Lady Mary always travelled in style, arriving at Callinafercy in a large four-wheeled carriage drawn by two meticulously groomed horses with gleaming polished harnesses. Her coachman, who was something of a dandy, with a stylish moustache which was carefully waxed and pointed at the ends, wore a tall Caroline hat and a long green coat trimmed

with gold buttons. Other visitors included Lady Edith
Gordon who had built the Elizabethan-style manor-house
of Ard na Sidhe at Caragh Lake, the Blennerhassetts from
Ballyseedy Castle near Tralee, the Crosbies from Ballyheigue,
the Cuffes from Caragh Lake, the O'Connells from Lakeview
near Killarney, and Sir Desmond and Lady Fitzmaurice from
Mount Rivers, Killorglin.

Another Godfrey house nearby was Glen Ellen, which
was built by James, third son of Sir John Godfrey, for his
bride, Mary Isabella Maunsell. Its later tenants included
Captain Lawrence Creigh-Howard, chief steward of the
Kilcoleman demesne, who was a leading light in the local
shooting fraternity. Every October, during the thirties and
forties, he organised one of the most prestigious shooting
parties of the year, which might take place on Kilcoleman
land, or at Callinafercy, or on the estate of Faha Court,
another great house near Listry, which had been built by
Morrogh Bernard, who had had his family crest and motto
inscribed over the great doorway; his love of horses is evident
from the large number of stables at Faha, which still survive.
After the day's shoot, the party usually returned to Glen
Ellen for a tumbler of warming whiskey punch or a glass
of full-blooded claret.

Other houses in the neighbourhood were Callinafercy
House, built by Anne Williams in 1841; Abbeylands, a
large and interesting eighteenth-century house, now radically
altered, which was the home of Seybourne May; and Ivy
Lodge, belonging to the Eagers—it was the birthplace of
Nano Eager who married Jeremiah O'Donovan Rossa, the
Fenian leader.

Weddings were great occasions, not only for the invited
guests but for the people of the area. When Kathleen Amy
King, a friend of the daughter of the house, May Leeson-
Marshall, married in Kilcoleman parish church in the
twenties, the wedding naturally made front page news in
the local paper:

The church was prettily decorated with heather and wild flowers. The bride wore a gown of ivory satin, her only ornament being an old pendant of emeralds, a gift of the bridegroom. Her veil of Honiton lace was fastened with a spray of myrtle and orange-blossom. She carried a bouquet of white carnations and white heather. Her four bridesmaids wore dresses of cream charmeuse, with transparent tunics bordered with gold. They also wore caps of white and gold lace and carried bouquets of red carnations. Their presents from the bridegroom were pendants of moonstone.

When May Leeson-Marshall married George Ansley Ruth in 1924, many of the local people gave eggs for the massive wedding-cake which was baked in Callinafercy. The great families from far and near were invited and a cortège of Ford motor cars took the wedding party to the small Church of Ireland chapel of Kilcoleman. The wedding reception was held in the drawing-room and dining-room at Callinafercy; a special butler was hired to help the resident butler with the arrangements and extra staff supplemented the home team. Local men patrolled the gates of the estate during the course of the reception to keep away any unwelcome intruders.

The tenants and workers had their own party in the farmhouse, near the back entrance to the estate. Any left-over cakes were given to the neighbours, and later they all received a small slice of wedding-cake in a box—each accompanied by a pretty card bearing the elegantly scripted names of the bride and groom.

At Callinafercy, my mother worked first as general kitchen-maid and assistant to the cook. Part of her duties included the milking by hand of six cows, morning and evening, and she was also responsible for boiling the water which was sent up to the Major's dressing-room where he shaved and dressed. The rest of the morning was spent in cleaning the various cooking utensils in the kitchen, in preparation for the arrival of the mistress who came regularly at twelve o'clock to discuss the menu for the day.

The staff took their meals in the servants' hall, a sombre wainscoted room at the back of the house. Cupboards in this room held the delph they used, while the china for the family was stored in the pantry beside the dining-room. Lunch for the family was at half-past one, dinner for the staff at two, tea at five, and dinner for the family at eight. The Marshalls had recently acquired a radio which was kept in the dining-room, but a connecting cable carried the sound to the servants' hall so that they could listen to the latest news from a loudspeaker placed on a side table.

As there was no basement in Callinafercy, the servants' bedrooms were on the top floor at the back of the house. Small and sparsely furnished, they were intended to hold two beds, two small wardrobes and perhaps a chair. However, the room which my mother shared with one of the maids was so small that one of the wardrobes was left permanently in the corridor. Most of the rooms had a little hearth for a fire, which kept the rooms warm in winter. The servants were allowed to sit in the servants' hall in the evening-time but the butler and his wife were usually the only ones who did, the other servants retiring to their rooms. As there were no radios (television was still a thing of the future) reading was the main activity. My mother was an avid reader of books such as *Jane Eyre*, *Wuthering Heights* and *Lorna Doone*.

Bathrooms had been installed in the house sometime before the twenties, but were for the use of members of the family only. The servants took baths in the privacy of their bedrooms, in old Victorian baths which had to be laboriously filled with kettles of hot water. When the baths were not in use they were left in the corridor near the servants' rooms.

In those days, servants had no regular days or half-days

off, the only free period being that which separated lunch and tea. But fresh scones were always required for tea, and if these had not been made before lunch they had to be made after it—which effectively cut out the leisure time. They did, however, get two weeks' annual holidays. There were occasional outings, usually to the beach at Rossbeigh; my mother's memories were mainly of the rain which was regularly an unforeseen and unwelcome feature of the chosen day. When the family dinner had been served and the dishes washed, long walks on lazy summer evenings, the skyline ablaze with the reddish tinge of the sinking sun, were a favourite pastime. One of the maids, a local girl, went home every evening and she thus enjoyed the excitement of walking to a country dance four or five miles away, while the other maids were confined to the house. They did, however, have some share of the action; any small piece of jewellery they might possess invariably went missing on the night of the dance.

When my mother first came to Callinafercy carriages were still in use, and she and the other servants travelled to mass in what was known as the back-to-back carriage. Later they travelled in the family car—rare things indeed in those days.

The most important figure in the household was Mr. Jones, the butler, who had responsibility for the cellar and the pantry, including the care of the silver. He also looked after the dogs—Rollo the great red setter, and Rose the golden retriever—who were housed at night in the kennels at the back of the cobbled yard.

In spite of his perception of the dignity of office, he had a sense of humour. Sometimes when the daily menu for the servants had become a little monotonous he would jokingly say to my mother (who had by then graduated to the position of cook), 'We'll have apples and rice for dessert today, and tomorrow, just for a change, we'll have rice and apples.' One of my mother's favourite stories about him concerned a lady guest who held the belief, common enough at the time, that everyone was born into a certain predetermined station in life. One afternoon while tea was being served in the drawing-room she expressed the opinion that the children of the gentry were the china of the world, while the servants and their offspring were merely common crockery. Mr. Jones, who had heard the remark, was shortly afterwards asked to send one of the servants to fetch some of the visiting children (who were only allowed into the reception rooms on special occasions) from their rooms upstairs, whereupon he shouted along the corridor to a maid, 'Crockery, go up and bring down the china.'

He was an admirer of the ill-fated Edward VIII of England and a picture of him, complete with fairisle sweater and dog, had pride of place on the pantry wall for a long time; it was judiciously removed after the abdication.

Mr. Jones was fond of shooting and liked nothing better than to stroll down along the riverbank on stormy winter evenings to shoot wild duck. He was also allowed to take the last day of the pheasant shoot as a free day, as a reward for having arranged the event. Some evenings he and his wife sat by the fire in the servants' hall listening to their old gramophone—mainly classical music but also some recordings by John McCormack. Other evenings they played cards or read the family newspaper, which made its way to the servants' hall when the Major had finished with it.

Mr. Jones's wife was the lady's-maid. She took complete charge of Mrs. Marshall's clothes, preparing dresses and gowns for special occasions, and helping her to dress. She spent most of the morning tidying away the clothes worn the previous day, coming downstairs about noon. After lunch she spent her time sewing and making alterations—lowering or raising a hemline, or adding a pretty lace collar to a plain black dress. Dress in those days was much more formal than it is now, with several changes of clothes through the day, and the servants were required to conform to the standards of 'upstairs'. The housemaids and parlour-maids changed their uniforms twice a day—blue and white in the morning, black and white in the evening.

Evening dinners, large or small, were ceremonial occasions. When the family and guests went to change into evening clothes, the butler also withdrew to dress himself in his swallow-tailed black suit and contrasting white shirt. The meal was cooked by my mother on the great iron range in the kitchen, each course being taken at regular intervals to the pantry, where it was passed through a hatch into the dining-room. A large decorative screen placed in front of the hatch allowed any last-minute adjustments to the appearance of the dishes to be made in privacy by the butler. A magnificent silver bowl filled with one of Mrs. Marshall's carefully composed flower arrangements was the focal point of the table when there were guests.

Soup, kept simmering in a pot for much of the day, was the first course. The main course ranged from roast beef or mutton to game birds or salmon. The latter, freshly caught in the River Maine and often received as a gift from one of the local families, was usually served simply—boiled or grilled cutlets—with an appropriate lemon sauce. My mother noted that the family liked their meat very rare while the servants preferred it well done. A succulent joint of roast pork was served with apple sauce, and in later years when we children objected to the bristle on a pork chop, my mother would invariably remind us that the Major took immense pleasure in eating pork bristle. Potatoes, mashed or roasted, would be accompanied by a wide range of vegetables, all home-grown—spinach, brocoli, beetroot, celery, radishes, curly kale, cauliflower, green beans, leeks and artichokes. Herbs were picked fresh from the garden. Afterwards there was a choice of fresh or bottled fruits; desserts like carmel custard, gooseberry fool or puffed sweet omelettes; or puddings such as apple dumplings, castle pudding, roly-poly pudding, bread and butter pudding, sultana pudding. In season there would be grapes from the greenhouse or figs from the tree in the back garden. Sometimes there might also be a cheeseboard before the final coffee course.

In common with most country estates, Callinafercy had a walled garden which grew choice fruits and flowers. When the fruit was ripe, it was picked by the servants and sorted into large bowls which were stored overnight in the larder. Next morning it was prepared for bottling or for making jam. The jams were cooked in a large preserving pan on the big range and transferred into jars, which were covered when cold. Cider was made from the apples and great earthenware jars were used to transport it to the workmen in the fields; these buff and beige jars kept it as cold as any modern refrigerator.

The dairy was another important centre of activity. There was a large herd of Kerry cows on the estate—sleek, diminutive, hardy, black animals which produced high milk yields. The milk was separated in a separator in the dairy at the back of the estate farmhouse. Then it was churned in a large barrel churn and the butter produced was weighed and packed in one pound portions. Creamed cottage cheese was sometimes made in small quantities. The buttermilk which remained after the churning process was used in baking soda bread and brown bread cakes.

When Major Marshall died in the late thirties my mother went with Mrs Leeson-Marshall to Kylemore House in Bray, County Wicklow, where she remained until 1944. On Mrs. Marshall's death, her sister-in-law, Margaret Hodson, gave my mother a letter of reference, which highlights the qualities then valued in a domestic servant. Dated 24 May, 1944, part of it read: 'She was for some years kitchen-maid under a good cook and then as cook till the present day. She understands all branches of cooking and makes excellent bread and cakes. She also understands dairy work and the making of butter.'

Now that domestic service is a thing of the past, it is worth recording that my mother did not consider her work was in any way degrading. Wages were invariably low but nevertheless the job offered a deep sense of security and self-esteem, as well as opportunities for promotion.

My mother remained in her next position at Ayesha Castle, Killiney, until the owners went to England in 1947. She came back to Callinafercy to be married that same year, and after her marriage she did occasional work for Mrs. Ruth, daughter of the Marshall household, who had inherited the house. It is from this time that my memories of Callinafercy date.

I often used to sit in the kitchen, watching while my mother prepared lunch or dinner. Sometimes I helped with cleaning the silver candelabras, teapots or kettles, or polishing the brass and copper service trays. Often in the stillness of a summer's day, the loudest sound in the kitchen would be the tick of the great-grandfather clock. But moments of calm were few. There were frantic moments when someone pulled the bell cord in the dining-room and the alarm rang loud along the corridor. Sauce jugs were hastily filled, plates quickly stacked, and vegetables placed in their bowls before being brought to the hatch in the pantry wall. Some of the dishes prepared were a source of wonder to me. The family regularly ate food that we would never dream of eating—things such as rabbits, snipe, woodcock or wild duck. My aunt said 'she was never done plucking for that woman in the big house.'

Mrs. Ruth was always feeding the little birds around the house with pieces of fat which she placed inside one half of an empty coconut. They grew very tame and cheeky, particularly the robins, who regularly flew in and out of the kitchen while my mother was at work, and the dogs were generally there too, lounging in their rushwork baskets on the floor. Mrs. Ruth said that if we were kind to animals they would never be afraid of us.

There were rare visits to the drawing-room which had an elegant if faded beauty. Geraniums—red and white and pink—were massed in the great bay window, which looked over the immaculate lawn and the great rhododendron, which in early summer shone like a glowing ruby in an emerald setting. The glittering chandelier, the old-fashioned harp, the grand piano, the sofa and armchairs with their faded print covers, the death-mask of Robert Emmet, the smiling portraits of long departed ancestors, the glass case of ornaments, the delicate blue vase on the mantelpiece— these are the images that stay in the mind.

The fragrance of roses hung on the air in the stately entrance hall, where a beautifully painted bowl, which stood on an hexagonal table, was filled with rose petals of creamy-white, pale pink and apricot. I remember the massive open fireplace surmounted by a gilt-edged mirror, an upright harmonium, the spreading antlers of a giant Irish elk over the door, and the sombre portrait of the first Earl of Milltown which hung on the wall above the floral chaise longue. The highly polished staircase led up to the family bedrooms, the guest rooms and the former nursery.

One of the things that never ceased to amaze me whenever I went to the great house was that the clocks—and there were clocks everywhere—usually showed contradictory times. If the hands of the grandfather clock in the kitchen pointed to half-past twelve, the clock on the upstairs landing invariably suggested that it was almost one o'clock. Meanwhile, the clock in the front hall was probably chiming noon, while the carriage clock on the table would indicate a quarter past one.

My first impressions of Mrs. Ruth were of a somewhat intimidating woman. She spoke in a highly cultured English accent, but if any visitor happened to comment on the fact she would profess amazement and declare herself to be totally Irish. She often became irritable when ordering groceries on the telephone, and if someone at the other end of the line failed to undertand her hastily given order immediately, she would proceed to spell the word with great deliberation and sarcasm. She would shout into the mouthpiece, 'I want a chicken—a C-H-I-C-K-E-N—if you know what that is.' She delighted in delaying the postman while she put the finishing touches to some vital piece of correspondence, which just had to be posted urgently. However, even though she could be temperamental at times, everyone who worked for her found that she could be satisfied easily. A visitor asked my aunt, who cleaned various rooms, if she was a hard taskmaster. 'Ereh, no, nor hard then,' was the answer. 'Sure the smell of the polish keeps her happy.'

Her favourite colours were varying shades of pale mauve, lilac and purple—colours that seemed to complement her skin tone. Walking her three Irish terriers to the avenue gates was part of her daily routine; she loved those dogs more than anything in the world and if one of them refused to obey a command she would say, 'Poor dear, she's as deaf as a post.' Her approach to gardening was highly inventive. Trees and shrubs had to be allowed to expand and develop when and where they wished. Any branches that overhung a garden pathway or encroached upon the avenue had to be propped up with a Y-shaped stick. To cut back or chop down anything was considered almost sacriligious. When gardening catalogues arrived reading them would be a morning's work, but she rarely ordered more than one or two packets of seeds.

Her approach to driving was—like her approach to gardening—eccentric to say the least. When she came to the avenue gates or the junction with the main Killorglin road she seldom took the trouble to look right or left; her black Prefect car would shoot gaily across the road! Amazingly, she never had an accident of any kind.

The females of the Marshall family were invariably late for everything, whether it was lunch, tea, dinner, or setting out on visits to friends, and Mrs. Ruth was no exception.

But she also maintained the family traditions in more positive ways. She continued to hold the children's summer party, with games, sack-races, egg-and-spoon races and a balloon Aunt Sally—balloons were tied on to a board and there were prizes for those children who managed to hit one with a small ball. There would be a lucky dip into a tea-chest, where little parcels lurked below layers of sawdust, and, afterwards, tea and cake in the dining-room.

Mrs. Ruth also upheld the family reputation for generosity to the poor, dispensing blankets, sheets and bedspreads whenever anyone was ill or when there was a death in the family. One local family that had suffered a bereavement was given a fine crochet bedspread and invited to keep it when the wake was over. She also established the custom of giving a wreath in honour of the deceased. The moment she heard of a death in the locality she went about the gardens, choosing flowers and shrubs to complement each other; in autumn and winter when flowers were scarce, she used foliage in all its various tints and textures. The country people were deeply impressed by her concern. They knew the time and effort that had gone into the making of the wreath, and the fact that she invariably came to present it to the family herself won her both respect and loyalty. She had her 'funny ould ways' they said—my aunt said she was 'full of branches' (meaning roguery)—but she 'was a good ould crathur at the back of it all'. She had great compassion for the bereaved and immediately offered any assistance that might be helpful, always in a sensitive, tactful way. All the neighbours turned to her in times of trouble because it was felt that she could 'put things better' than they could, and when my father died suddenly it was Mrs. Ruth who broke the tragic news to my mother. She offered not only sympathy but practical help; we had sold our only cow at that stage and she decided that we would be supplied with a free bottle of milk every day, courtesy of those beautiful Kerry cows that I admired so much. A jar of coins—

the old brown pennies with hens on them—was kept on the kitchen table, specially set aside for members of the travelling community who might call. She was keenly interested in local events. People from Milltown always went to her for flowers for the Corpus Christi procession in June, and she sent them away with huge masses of blooms and garlands of leaves.

Nor did she scoff at local folklore. In fact, she liked to feel that she too was part of that rich and colourful heritage. When a spoon or knife went missing temporarily, she would declare that the fairies had taken it and would return it as soon as they had finished with it. On Easter Sunday morning it was her custom to rise early to see the sun dance in the heavens, and she never forgot to ask us children if we had seen it too. There was a rookery behind the old yellow-washed farmhouse, and she told us that every year the crows left Callinafercy for three days in September when they set out for Galway races.

Miss Phyllis Godfrey of Kilcoleman Abbey was one of the many visitors who came to visit Mrs. Ruth. She was a decidedly impatient lady, continually blaring the horn of her old Ford car at horse-drawn carts, especially those loaded down with hay, which were generally so wide that they occupied the entire breath of the narrow road. My grandmother and most of her contemporaries regarded people like Miss Phyllis with something bordering on reverential awe. When anyone became ill, my grandmother would declare that the person had a 'fit of cold' or 'a fit of rheumatism' or 'a fit of stomach trouble'. Once when Miss Phyllis had a cold, my grandmother presented her respects when she reappeared in public again and, feeling obliged to make discreet enquires about the great lady's health, said to her, 'And how're you after your fit, ma'am?' Miss Phyllis stared in amazement, wrinkled her forehead and replied dourly, 'My good woman, none of the Godfreys ever got a fit.' She strode away, leaving my grandmother feeling rather bruised, more certain than ever that people like the Godfreys did not speak the same language as she did—though she often laughed about it afterwards.

Whenever we sighted a huge flock of pigeons rising suddenly skywards from among the trees at Callinafercy we immediately knew that Captain Popoff had come to stay. One of his greatest pleasures was to clap his hands as loudly as he could and frighten the birds into flight. He often asked us children if we could speak Irish, invariably finishing with *Oiche Mhaith* (Good night), which we suspected were the only words of Irish he knew.

Another visitor was Mrs. Leeson, who always made what seemed to us to be extravagant claims about the amount of property once owned by the family; they had at one time, she assured everyone, owned the whole of Leeson Street in Dublin. Every time she visited Callinafercy, the colour of her hair had changed yet again, which was of course a rare and strange event in those days, and far more talked about by us than her territorial claims.

Dean Grey Stack of Kenmare was also a regular, and occasionally there was a continental visitor or two. Elsa, a Finnish girl, came to stay with Mrs. Ruth one summer, and much to the latter's delight she married the local rector, Reverend Warren. A German family, the Stellmarks, who were evacuees from Germany during World War II, spent much of that time at Callinafercy, and returned to visit in later years.

My mother and I took regular walks along the avenue in spring to admire the great masses of daffodils growing at the base of the three great oak-trees in the adjoining field, appropriately known as the 'Three Oaks'. At Eastertime there was the spreading cherry-tree laden with double snow-white blossoms, and close by, on the back avenue, another with ice-pink blooms. In summer, the purple rhododendrons, as well as the more exotic pink and red varieties,

were masses of gaudy colour. The pendant pink blossoms
of the ornamental fuchsia shook in the light summer wind,
and the drone of the honey bees filled the air. The spreading
beech-trees were canopies of green which filtered the sunlight
or, on rainy days, their branches dripping and moist, they
were still magnificently beautiful. Holly-trees scattered here
and there gave a dark, rich, lustrous glow to the wood,
but my favourites were the speckled laurels.

Our little brown donkey was allowed to graze on the
estate and was something of a favourite with Mrs. Ruth.
Somehow he seemed to remind her of the time when the
estate had been home to a large number of horses and ponies.
Sometimes on summer days we could see him skulking inside
the thickets of rhododendron that grew in the centre of
one of the avenue fields. Mrs. Ruth, too, knew of his hiding-
place. 'He looks at me roguishly,' she would whisper as
if confiding a great secret. 'And do you know what I think
he is saying? He is saying, "If you see anyone looking for
me, don't tell them that I'm in here." '

One of the most beautiful times of the year was the

autumn, when clouds of leaves drifted to earth, littering the avenue with brown and orange and yellow and russet, all rustling and crackling underfoot. It was the time too for pine cones, which we called gigs.

In winter, when the scarlet berries were on the holly-trees, our thoughts turned to ghosts, and coming home through the gloaming we would remember the stories of mysterious horses and carriages which came and went unseen through the stillness and the shadows. A neighbour remembered a day in the twenties when, as a boy, he and his father waited at the back of the house for the return of the Major in the horse and trap—it was his father's job to tend the horse. Suddenly, they heard the sound of horses' hooves and carriage-wheels but when they went out into the yard there was nothing to be seen. Yet the sinister sound of galloping hoofbeats and the trundling of wheels over the cobblestones continued for some time around the deserted stable yard.

We often visited the doll's house and were told that people on the run had sheltered in it during the turbulent days of the Civil War. Much of the fine fretwork had been torn down since then by people who had heard these stories and who hoped that guns might have been left behind.

A favourite haunt of ours was the fort overlooking Dingle Bay. We rested in the shadow of its walls or explored its fosse and mound, while our brown and white sheepdog danced on daisies and clover in the silly pursuit of a seagull soaring gracefully in the skies high above. We went to see the old windmill, also part of local folklore because it had been lowered nine or ten feet in 1928 when it was found that the sails were taking in too much wind.

Today the big house stands apart, in splendid but sad isolation, no longer the focal point of a closely knit community, but quite distinct and removed from it, the social fabric that underpinned it having been torn asunder.

The Marshalls no longer live at Callinafercy. That era came to a close with the death of Mrs. Ruth in 1988. She was buried beside her husband beneath a handsome Celtic cross in the graveyard in the grounds of the Church of Ireland church in Milltown. She had long been a passionate supporter of her local church, some would say even a champion, and it was only at the time of her death that I learned that she had had another remarkable claim to fame; she had been the first woman to be elected to the General Synod of the Church of Ireland. Appropriately, her funeral service was conducted entirely through the medium of Irish. She was a great lover of the language and many of her favourite hymns and carols were in Irish. Her husband, too, had been a fluent speaker and had taught in an Irish college in Dublin. Mrs. Ruth visited the Blasket Islands a number of times and amongst the people she knew there was Máire Ni Ghuithín, who mentions in her book *Bean an Oileáin* that the first time she ever saw a red squirrel was in the woods of Callinafercy.

I made a wreath for her, a small token of appreciation for the many wreaths she had so lovingly wrought for bereaved families in the area. But though they are gone, to me the voices of the family still echo and their memory lingers on.

6
School and Holidays

The first school that I went to was the local national school, which had been built in 1888 in the traditional style. The windows were distinctively Irish in character—tall and narrow with small panes of glass—set in roughcast stone walls. It was built with monies from the Commissioners' Grant and the Fitzgerald Fund and replaced one that had been established some ten years before—interestingly I came across the entry for my grandmother from the roll-books of this older school, still preserved in all its meticulous detail:

Date of Entrance:	9th October 1883
Register Number:	133
Name of Pupil:	Kate Clifford
Address:	The Cliff
Age of Pupil last Birthday:	5
Religious Denomination:	R.C.
Means of living of parent:	Labourer

In the records of the 1888 school, the majority of parents whose children attended the school were listed as labourers, farmers or fishermen. Among the more unusual occupations were those of a gatekeeper, a cooper, a tailor, a few army pensioners, a railway worker and a civic guard (RIC).

In September 1889, Major Marshall wrote that he was 'much pleased with the general appearance of the place and the neatness of the scholars'. Fifteen years later the parish priest, Father Carmody, commented that he was 'very pleased that the children had a little Irish'. The principal at the school at that time was Jamsie Lambe, and one old neighbour recalled that it was his avowed intention 'to ensure that Callinafercy was the best national school within a radius of forty miles'.

Sixty or so years on, when I made my first appearance there, scholastic achievement was still highly prized. Possibly the place was a lot more cheerful than in the old days. I remember that the walls were painted buttercup yellow, with the woodwork in a lively shade of brown. There was an open fireplace in two of the three class-rooms, and in the wintertime, when the fire blazed in the grate, we placed our bottles of cocoa and milk near it to warm them. One or two children were regularly sent each day to a nearby farmhouse to fetch a bucket of water for the master's tea. I dreaded being sent because we sometimes encountered an old man with a dog, who for some strange reason frightened the wits out of me.

English, Irish and arithmetic were the main subjects on the curriculum. We had no formal textbooks for history or geography, nor did we need any. For the schoolmaster, Murt Kelly, sitting on the edge of one of the long desks, hands clasped firmly together, told us stories that made the history of Ireland more exciting and alive than all the words contained between the covers of any dull book ever could. These stories, collectively referred to as *stair*, were interlaced with colour, adventure and no little humour. We gloried in the triumphs of the great Brian Boru, particularly his victory at Clontarf. We lamented the fate of the heroic Wild Geese, heard of the dreams of Tone and Emmet, the tragedy of the famine, the genius of Davitt and the vision of 1916. Probably as a result, two of my favourite characters in Irish history were Padraig Pearse and Thomas Ashe. My mother often said that Murt Kelly was 'a grand man', and that he was, for not only did he have knowledge to impart but he did so with enthusiasm.

In those pre-fountain-pen days we wrote with pens which had to be dipped into ink-wells. When the master's back was turned, or when he was busy checking attendance figures in the roll-book, we would slowly lift the ink-wells and symbolically drink a toast to some distant dream, like chips for tea or no Irish spellings for the week-end. All our lessons in geography were, in fact, conducted through the medium of Irish. A large map of Ireland hung on one wall and Murt Kelly would stand near it, calling on some child to point out Letterkenny or Belmullet, while he himself craftily stared at some point on the east coast in an effort to confuse the poor victim. Compositions were my favourite subject and we were usually asked to write about country things like 'Setting the Potatoes', 'A Fair Day', 'A Day in the Bog' and 'The Thresher'.

The dreaded inspector came from time to time, and very happy we were indeed when he confined himself to talking to the master in fluent Irish. There were fervent preparations for Communion and Confirmation, with the trauma of an unfamiliar priest arriving to make sure we knew the meanings of words such as Incarnation, Salvation and Purgatory; we hard-pressed students of religion were wont to declare that we had first-hand experience of the latter. In the twenties and thirties each child was given a ticket by the parish priest when he or she was deemed to have passed the catechism examination. The child took this ticket to the church with him; without it apparently he could not be confirmed. Inside the church the bishop then moved amongst the rows and questioned certain children at random. My aunt Kathy told me that on one such confirmation day, Jamsie Lambe cycled past some Callinafercy children, who were making their way, heads stuffed with all the knowledge contained in Power's Manual and Catechism Notes, to Milltown church. 'Do your best,' he urged them. 'I hear the bishop tore up a pile of tickets in Brosna the other day.'

Bishops were not, indeed, our favourite characters. We heard dreadful stories about temperamental specimens who, in the midst of calm and serenity, would abruptly pose a trick question such as 'Name the seven deadly sins'. Not only that; these bishops sometimes went so far as to eject acolytes forcibly from the chapel; and the ceremonial slap on the cheek had been known to knock boys flat on their backs at the altar rails, where they lay prostrate, objects of derision for the assembled multitude. Those were stirring times, with a long list of Do's and Dont's. I was suitably mortified, having received Holy Communion several times with my cap still on my head, to find that this was considered sacrilegious.

But there were light-hearted moments, too. We had regular singing classes, when we sang songs such as *An Poc ar Buile*, *Thugamar Féin an Samhradh Linn* and *Peigi Leitir Mhór*; on a more serious note our songs included *Boolavogue*, *Deep in Canadian Woods* and *The Foggy Dew*.

We always had a special welcome for the wandering showmen and magicians, who were ready and willing to provide impromptu shows at the cost of sixpence per head. One of these gentlemen had a 'magic oven' which would instantly produce any food selected from a pack of cards, each of which bore the name of a different food; the success of the 'magic' depended upon the co-operation of the schoolmaster to ensure that certain cards were chosen and certain others excluded. Itinerant photographers occasionally appeared, who fixed their cameras on three-pronged pedestals and disappeared under black cloths saying, 'Ready! Smile!'

Members of clerical orders made regular visits and pointed out the attractions of their religious life, but most of their premises were beyond our understanding. The brother or sister who gave the talk usually concluded by asking who would like to join their order, promptly visiting the home of any child who expressed an interest. A few such visits were made, but the religious fervour soon wore off and all was calm once more. More easily understood and enjoyed were the children's pages of magazines such as *Africa* and *The Far East*—a particular favourite was the ever-popular Pudsy Ryan, whose inventive approach to spelling was something which struck a sympathetic chord. Images of black babies were constantly on our minds and we were always collecting for some mission or other, the mite or collection box being a regular feature in most homes.

As the school was near a wood this was our regular play

area, and here we played games that probably went back for generations. The tall pines provided excellent goal-posts and were perfect for 'Corners', a game where each of four players stood near a tree, with one player in the centre. When his back was turned the players would quickly change places. If he was alert enough and quick enough he would succeed in getting to a vacant corner first. The ousted player then became 'centre'.

In 'Willie Willie Wagtail' the players formed a line at a given starting-point, while the leader stood some distance away with his back turned towards the others. He then recited, 'Willie Willie Wagtail, one, two, three, four ...' stopping whenever he chose and turning around suddenly. Any player caught moving was ordered back to the starting line. The player clever enough to reach the leader first was declared the new leader.

The game of 'Colours' required a 'devil', an 'angel' and other players. First, each player was secretly given a different colour. The devil knocked two stones together, and the angel answered, 'Come in,' asking the devil what he wanted. 'Colours,' the devil would reply. 'Name the colours,' the angel would demand. The obliging devil would recite various colours. When he happened to call out a colour assigned to a player, this player stepped forward and was chased by the devil. If he was caught before the end of a certain time lapse, he or she would go to hell; if the player eluded the clutches of the devil, he or she would go to heaven. When all the players had been allocated, the game began again.

Conversation and rhyme was an essential part of 'Grandmother Gray', a game often played in the forties by girls:

Children:	Grandmother Gray, may we go out to play?
Grandmother:	See is the day fine.
Children:	The sun is splitting the stones.

<pre>
Grandmother: Don't go with boys,
               Don't smoke fags,
               Don't hunt the ducks.
</pre>

The girls then went outside and, like all mild-mannered children, immediately pretended to go with boys, smoke fags and hunt the ducks, which made Grandmother Gray lose her patience:

<pre>
Grandmother: Children! Children!
   Children: We don't hear you.
Grandmother: Where are your manners?
   Children: In my shoe.
Grandmother: Whom do you care for?
   Children: Not for you.
</pre>

At this stage Grandmother Gray would lose all patience with her brood and run around trying to catch them.

Another rhyme-and-conversation game was 'The Old Woman from Jubilee Land', in which the players were the Old Woman, another woman, and children. The Old Woman began:

> Here comes an old woman from Jubilee Land,
> With forty small children by her hand.
> Each one can knit, each one can sew;
> Each one can make a lily-white bow,
> Each one can make a bed for the Queen,
> So please take one of my daughters.

The other woman, being a kind-hearted soul, willingly accepted one of the children. The Old Woman from Jubilee Land then went coyly away, apparently quite happy to have abandoned one of her progeny, but she soon returned to repeat the same rhyme over and over again, until she had got rid of all her children.

Domestic accomplishments were also mentioned in a game, popular in the Milltown area, which concerned the fate of poor Jenny Joe:

Jenny Joe, Jenny Joe. How is she now?
    She's washing clothes, washing clothes,
    And you can't see her now.
Jenny Joe, Jenny Joe. How is she now?
    She's sick in the bed,
    And she can't see you now.

The Kerry gift of repartee was often born in the school-yard. My brother remembers this little incident:

Once when the lads were playing in the yard, one fellow was wearing a cap. Jerry Sullivan, who lived at the railway gates, took the cap and threw it up on the roof of the school. When the master came out, he asked how the cap had found its way on to the roof. 'It fell up, sir,' said Jerry, quick as a flash.

So much for the laws of gravity in Callinafercy!

My best friend at school was Michael O'Sullivan of Bansha, Killorglin, whose father was also a fisherman. Other good friends were my next-door neighbours, Billy, Jerry and Donal McKenna, while their older brother Johnny was best friends with my brother. I was always reading comics and books after school, sometimes getting through the complete comic I had bought in Killorglin, on the journey home from the fishery office. I wrote little stories, too, inspired by my mother, though the poor woman often joked that everything she said fell on deaf ears when I had my head in the books.

Michael O'Sullivan and I wrote little magazines exclusively for one another; readership—one per issue! These contained a great deal of information about the showband circuit, information which we either gleaned from older sisters and brothers or from *New Spotlight* magazine, which was the rage of the age in the early sixties. It was filled with photos of showbands such as the Dixies, the Cadets, the Royal and the Miami, who were also featured on the sponsored radio programmes of the time. My favourite, however, was Butch Moore, and I still have in my possession an autographed photo of him from those days.

My sister Catherine had little or no interest in school. When she went to the Vocational School in Killorglin she found the headmaster's suggestion that she should spend three hours at her homework each night quite hilarious. One of her greatest diversions was letting the air out of one of the wheels of her bicycle so that she could enjoy an extended chat with her friends on the road home from Killorglin. The father of one of this illustrious circle was wont to declare rather dramatically, 'I'll wear the soles off my shoes to keep my Margaret goin' to that school.' My sister, however, had no interest in higher education, and after two years there she went to work in an hotel in Killarney.

If I was interested in books, and my sister had an ingrained aversion to them, my brother Johnny was very much into football, which has always been regarded as a religion in Kerry. Our teacher Murt Kelly had played football at county level for both Dublin and Kerry, and even games in the school-yard were taken very seriously indeed. As I belonged to that rarest of all species—a Kerry boy who could not play football—I was invariably picked last when it came to the selection of the teams. I think I was rather philosophical about it, because, as my mother would have said, a fellow couldn't be good at everything! My brother, on the other hand, was so good that he won dozens of medals, going on to captain the local Milltown team and even getting a trial game for the Kerry minors. He was not the only enthusiast in the family; my father cycled regularly to matches on Sundays, and enjoyed a pint in the pub afterwards—at Coffeys in Killorglin, or Larkins or Langfords in Milltown.

My interests were somewhat more trivial. The moss in the bogs near the school held a particular fascination for

Mike and me. We collected the different coloured mosses and used them to represent rooms in an imaginary house under the shade of the trees. These mossy rooms were a patchwork quilt of colour and textures—reds and greens and golden-yellows. Occasionally during our searches we managed to fall into one or other of the bog-holes, which fortunately were not very deep. If this happened during school term, we were sent home, looking so dark and black that a little gospel music would not have been inappropriate.

Making 'spillers' was another pastime. These consisted of a length of fishing line, with hooks and worms attached at various points, looped round two nails on a plank of wood; a stone anchored the line in place. When we set the spiller the line was unwound and hurled out across the tide in the ordinary way. There were tiny little pools along the strand, and when the tide went out it left minute little fish stranded in the pools. We collected these 'pinkeens' in jam jars.

One of the less pleasant episodes of my childhood happened one evening when I was cycling a bicycle which belonged to a friend, and which was missing one of its pedals. The metal shaft of the holder ripped through the side of my left knee, leaving a long and bloodied wound in its wake. News of my misfortune travelled fast, for I had scarcely been helped back home by my brother and sister when many of the neighbours gathered round. My mother wrapped a clean white cloth round the unsightly wound, which seemed to me to be spewing blood at a furious rate. Mrs. Ruth appeared on the scene. She had had some nursing experience, but having inspected the damage she suggested that it would be best to wait for the doctor. When he came and began to stitch the wound, having carried out the necessary preliminaries, the neighbours still stood about the kitchen, carefully observing his every move at a respectful distance. It was as if Doctor Sheehan and I were the principal players in an absorbing drama and the neighbours were our audience. I vividly remember the grimaces on the faces of some of the observers, but curiously I felt reassured by their presence. When the drama was over, I discovered that being an invalid had distinct advantages; I was very happy at school but this unscheduled holiday was more than welcome. One of the aspects of that 'holiday' that I remember most clearly is watching the workers on the road laying the pipes for the piped water supply which was to herald the end of those unforgettable walks to the well.

Both at school and in the holidays, nature was all round us. In May and June we could hear the wandering voice of the cuckoo as we pondered imponderables such as 'If it took seven men three days to build a bridge, how many days would it take ten men to build the same bridge.' We heard the twitter of the swallows and the raucous squawking of the crows who came to the yard in search of crusts and crumbs after lunch. The squabbling of the herons in the tree-tops was one of the most familiar sounds of the forest world, and we often met the flock of guinea–fowl which wandered into the woods from the nearby estate, or disturbed the colourful pheasants with their distinctive call, as they stalked through the ferns and bracken. There were fleeting glimpses of the russet fox scurrying through the undergrowth; my mother often told us a story about three little foxes who were frightened by a malicious old hound, and I often imagined that the fox we saw in the woods might have been one of them.

The countryside around us was full of goldfinches and we admired the clever knack they had of extracting seeds from the tops of thistles. Once we tried to catch one. A friend had acquired a sticky paste he called bird-lime, and we applied this to a few twigs in the hope that the birds would perch on them and become embedded in the paste. We spent several hours watching and waiting but caught nothing; I was glad because the goldfinches looked so happy and contented in their own little world out-of-doors.

In the summertime bird-nesting was a favourite pastime and how delighted we were to find a speckled thrush in her nest among the tangled bine stems or two little wren's eggs in a nest in a mossy bank. But we were careful not to disturb anything—my mother told us that if we even breathed too closely on the eggs the birds might desert the nest and never return. Our neighbour Mary often joined us after school when we went collecting firewood in the grove near our cottage. She delighted in extricating broken branches and twigs from awkward positions at great height, paying little attention to those that crackled underfoot. We children were given the task of collecting the smaller sticks, called *kippins* or *brosna*, while Mary and my mother kept the larger branches for themselves.

In the autumn we children were out in 'armies', picking blackberries along the hedgerows or in the fields. We sold them to a local shopkeeper who stored them in old-fashioned timber barrels, to be later delivered to blackberry merchants for use in dyeing processes. We were paid by weight and, alas, some few were not averse to occasionally adding a little water to the juice of the berries to add more bulk. One old man who owned a field by the river bank was a born exaggerator and when he met us on the road with our blackberry cans, he would urge us to go into his field, saying, 'The berries are so heavy there, boys, ye'll milk 'um into the jars.' We would later discover that the field held not a single berry. 'It must have been d'oul wind d'other night,' he would explain philosophically. 'Sure 'tid shake the nose off a Moses himself.'

Harvest time also meant a few desperate and quite daring attempts to steal an apple or two from a neighbour's orchard. When we were caught, as we invariably were, a lecture on the immorality of stealing made us promise to reform our wicked ways, but the sight of those yellowing apples—'sheep-faces', the orchard owner called them—was a temptation we could rarely resist.

In those days, cigarettes had no health warning attached. Smoking had a certain adult status attached to it and the fact that it was forbidden fruit made it seem all the more attractive. On more than one occasion, when a friend and I had made persistent nuisances of ourselves, some of the older lads would provide us both with the very butt of a cigarette, adding sternly that they didn't want to see us for the rest of the evening. On long hot summer twilights, lazy curls of smoke drifted slowly skywards as we puffed and blew to our heart's content behind an old haystack. The sensation was delicious—but my mother later declared that it was a miracle from God that we hadn't set the entire place alight.

Riddles were in widespread circulation among school children in my time, and were often related to the life we led. *Riddle*: 'What is under the fire, over the fire and never touches the fire?' *Answer*: A cake of bread in a pot oven. *Riddle*: 'What is the black sheep with the white fleece?' *Answer*: A griddle with a cake of bread baking on top. *Riddle*: 'A polly-cow tied to the wall; she drinks all she gets and eats nothing at all!' *Answer*: An oil lamp. *Riddle*: 'I came on the back of a person and went out as soft as silk.' *Answer*: Turf. *Riddle*: 'Long legs, crooked thighs, small head and no eyes.' *Answer*: A tongs. *Riddle*: 'Long-legged father, big-bellied mother, three little children all the same colour.' *Answer*: A three-legged pot and pot hangers.

My mother's favourite was: 'What is full and holds more?' *Answer*: A pot of potatoes.

Household items also figured as subjects. *Riddle*: 'Janey white petticoat, with a long nose; the longer she lives, the shorter she grows.' *Answer*: A candle. *Riddle*: 'Two little girls dressed in white; one got a fit and died last night.' *Answer*: Two candles, one of which has been quenched. *Riddle*: 'A hard-working father; a lazy old mother; twelve little children, all the same colour.' *Answer*: a clock.

Riddles about birds, animals and fruit were favourites

of mine: 'As black as ink; as white as milk; it hops on
the road like hailstone.' *Answer:* A magpie.

> Up the green valley and down a green path,
> Ladies and gentlemen, tread upon that.
> Some with green gowns, some with green caps,
> And you're a good scholar if you'll riddle me that.
>   *Answer:* Ducks and drakes.

> As white as milk, and milk it is not.
> As green as grass, and grass it is not.
> As red as blood, and blood it is not,
> As black as ink, and ink it is not.
>   *Answer:* A blackberry.

The summer holidays always meant a visit to my mother's
native place—Claodach. We generally hired a car but once
or twice, when the Yanks and some neighbours went with
us, we rose to a bus. Our more usual travelling companions
were Aunt Rita and Cousin James. We visited three houses
in the one day—those of Aunt Lucy, Uncle Frank and Uncle
Timmie, the latter being the old homestead, where the
pendulum clock, with the spider's web elegantly traced on
its glass door, still beat time on the wall of the kitchen.
As we travelled along my mother and Rita talked about
old times, mentioning colourful place-names such as
Cumeenabhric, which means the badger's glen, and
Knocknabró. The mountains looked fabulous on those sunny
days, with purple splashes of heather scattered here and
there.

The old home was always the last port of call and though
we had already stuffed ourselves at Lucy's and Frank's we
somehow found room for more, for Timmie and his wife
Nora insisted on giving us a grand spread too. Part of the
ritual of the visit to the old home was the drinking of water
from the crystalline stream that flowed down the mountain
close to the house. There was no purer water in Kerry,

my mother and Rita assured one another with great conviction, as they savoured the waters of their youth once again. Amongst the dripping boulders in the stream were wonderful rosettes of St. Patrick's cabbage *(saxifraga spathularis)*, a plant known as London Pride in some places, but apparently not found in Britain.

Some years there was time for glimpses of the Marshall's hunting-lodge, a great pink building, with a red and white dresser in the kitchen and green shutters on the windows. One of the many jugs on the dresser was a gilded pink one bearing the word 'Killorglin', which had apparently been purchased by one of the caretakers of the lodge at a fair.

There were other days out during the summer—perhaps a bus trip to Tralee or to Rossbeigh—but nothing could compare with those magical visits to family and friends in Claodach of the purple hills.

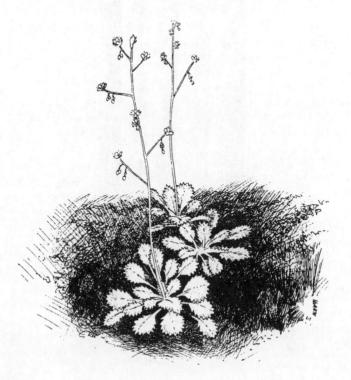

7
Echoes of the Past

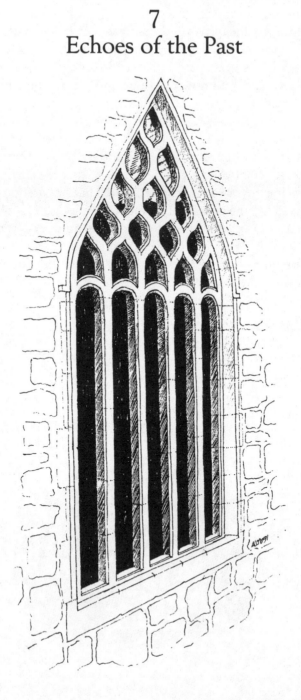

At some point in time, history and legend become inextricably intertwined and it is difficult to separate hard fact from the colourful folk memories handed down from generation to generation, usually by word of mouth, that embroidered these facts. Milltown and Callinafercy are no exceptions to this rule.

Many Kerry legends record the intervention of birds in the siting of an abbey or monastery. Killagha Abbey was to be sited in the townland of *Farranamanagh* ('land of the monks'), near Milltown, but when building was about to begin a great flock of crows appeared and transported all the masonry and tools to Killagha. This mysterious occurrence was interpreted as a sign from heaven and the Abbey was built on the site selected by the crows.

Many of the old ivy-clad churches in the neighbourhood (now used only as burial-places) were said to have been destroyed in Cromwellian times. There is a story that when Killagha Abbey was attacked by Cromwellian forces, the monks removed the precious bell from the bell-tower and hurled it into the depths of a nearby pool. Scarcely had it disappeared than the waters turned brilliant blue and from that day forth it was known as *poll gorm* or the blue pool. Later on, when the waters took on a brownish coloration, this was said to be the rust from the great bell; in those romantic days there was no thought of pollution.

Killagha was celebrated for the magnificence of its architecture. Local tradition records that in the early 1800s a sea captain, having heard of the splendours still to be found in the ruins of the Abbey, arrived from nearby Castlemaine where the cargo of his ship had been unloaded. During the night he and his crew hacked away a section of the intricate tracery around the mullioned Gothic east window and had taken to sea before the damage was discovered. Later that day, however, a great storm erupted and it was felt that this was a form of retribution sent by heaven to punish the sailors for their sacrilege.

If Cromwellian forces were blamed for the destruction of the Abbey of Killagha they were also credited with the origins of Puck Fair:

> When Cromwell's soldiers were raiding Ireland, a large number were on a mission in Kerry. The troopers were coming over the Kerry mountains and making for Killorglin and when traversing Carran Tuathail, a flock of goats grazing on the side of the mountain were affrighted by the presence of the soldiers. They made helter-skelter for Killorglin, other flocks joining in the stampede, and never stopped till they reached the town, into which they dashed madly, headed by a great puck. The inhabitants were alerted to the danger and assembling in strength they were ready when the soldiers showed up, to beat them—which they did. To record their perpetual gratitude to the puck for saving their lives it was decided to honour the horned defender of the town by dedicating a fair to him.

The woods of Killacloghane near Milltown reverberate with echoes of penal times, because it was here that the local mass rock was situated. When all forms of Catholic worship were forbidden, priests and people gathered at the rock to celebrate mass in this lonely little wood. It was at Killacloghane, in 1655, that Father Thaddeus Moriarty, a Dominican friar from Tralee, celebrated his last mass. Father Moriarty, a brother-in-law of the West Kerry poet and patriot, Piaras Feiritéir, was arrested at the rock and taken to the dungeons of Ross Castle on the shores of the lakes of Killarney. He was later hanged from the scaffold on Martyrs' Hill in Killarney.

Daniel O'Connell (1775-1847), the hero of Catholic emancipation, figures prominently in Milltown tradition. Once when travelling from Derrynane in West Kerry to Dublin, the celebrated Dan spent a night in the local inn, the Godfrey Arms Hotel in the village square, and a local resident, Denis Sugrue, had in his possession a pipe which he is reputed to have left behind. Another link with O'Connell was the large and beautiful tree which stood in the square; older people are adamant that this had been planted by Dan during his stay in Milltown.

O'Connell also passed through Castlemaine and a local poet, Sylvester Shea, composed some verses in his honour. Sadly only one verse was still remembered in the forties:

> Thrice welcome, brave O'Connell,
> Our guiding star through bondage drear.
> Who freed us without ransom
> From torture and from galling chains.
> Who wrought Emancipation,
> Against the tyrants made a stand.
> And now in spite of fate,
> He'll gain Repeal for Paddy's land.

Alas, as history records, O'Connell never did accomplish the Repeal of the Union.

The great famine of 1847 was a devastating event in the history of Ireland and the memory of those terrible times lingered long in the folk culture of the people. Two Welsh clergymen who visited Callinafercy during the famine period left this record:

> The natives of this region are very badly off and are the picture of misfortune. Many live rather more like animals than people. We saw one family living in a hole at the side of a large bank by a river and we were astonished to discover an ugly old woman on the side of the road creeping out of a sort of hut similar to a dog's kennel. As we were going by foot, we had more occasion to see the huts. They were very dirty at the side of the dykes, about as large and of the same structure as a Welsh farmer's potato pit.

A phenomenon of the famine times was the establishment

of 'soup kitchens'. The soup was prepared in massive cauldrons and dispensed to all comers—provided that they transferred their allegiance to some Protestant sect.

One of the fields near Callinafercy House is still known as *Pairc na Soupers* and it was here that a Miss Banks set up her soup kitchen. She came from Edinburgh at the height of the famine, and decided that the best way to help the natives was to impart agricultural skills, together with religious instruction. She acquired an old stables and barn, which she converted into a schoolhouse. She also rented some land which she cultivated herself as an example to the surrounding countryside, but no assistance was given to anyone who did not accept soup from her kitchen. Her activities gave rise to enormous tensions in the local community as the starving peasants had to choose, literally, between body and soul. As a child I heard stories of how Catholic priests had dragged local children, by the ears, from Miss Banks's school. To retain the loyalty of their flocks, priests in the Milltown area frequently threatened to change the children of offending parents into hares and hounds and set the latter on the former. The Presbyterian ministers responded to this threat by guaranteeing that they would change the children back into their normal state again.

A minister of a Protestant sect, the Rev. Boite, who lived at Callinafercy House about the 1850s, was widely known as something of an eccentric. At one party in his house, it was recorded that the Protestant guests dined in the parlour while the priests dined with the hounds. Another version of the story was told to me by Bob Knightly, who lived close to *Pairc na Soupers*:

The minister was having a party one Friday and when the priest came he was horrified to see plate after plate of mate (meat) on the table. 'The dogs of the house would not ate mate today,' said the priest. But the minister only laughed. Then the priest put down a plate of mate before the dogs and the dogs gathered round but they wouldn't look at the mate. The priests had the biteen of power, you know.

It is interesting to note that, whatever their differences, minister and priest were at least on visiting terms!

A few days later, according to legend, the minister travelled to Cork and the priests told the people that he was going for a rope—to hang himself. Sometime after his return, Rev. Boite did, in fact, commit suicide and was found hanging from one of the trees in the orchard. His body was buried in Killagha, which had been a Catholic graveyard before the suppression of the monasteries, but it was dug up during the night. It was reburied, only to be dug up a second time. This happened again and again until it was finally decided to hurl the body over the bank into the River Maine, and there is still an inlet marked on the map called *Cluisin Boite*, where the body apparently floated in with the tide at regular intervals.

My father was one of the many local men who repaired the river banks during the fifties and he told me that the more superstitious amongst them were never too keen on working close to the inlet on dark winter evenings.

Another old man remembered the closure of the Protestant school at Callinafercy House:

My father brought down boxes full of roll-books and slates and slate pencils. He took two boxes of them over to Dr. Myles in Inch. We (the children) were in dread to go near the slates and slate pencils because the priests had warned us against them.

In the sixties we met people who had seen the great soup cauldrons, and we heard tell of people who had come to gape at the noose hanging from the apple-tree where the minister had hanged himself. An Irish song about the soupers was sung in Callinafercy in the twenties:

Tháinig seana bhean anuas on Albain,
Go raibh peidhre mhaidi croise aici;
Ni raibh fiacal in a ceann na raibh ar sionna crith;
Druidfidh uaim amach go mbuailfeadh dhá bhuille
  orthu-
Taimse im chodladh is ná dústear mé
Mar ar Aonach a Phocan, ne leomhfaidh siad seasamh
  ann,
Ná gabháil tríd an tsráid a rása na gcapall ann;
Taimse im chodladh is ná dústear mé.
Bhí Seamas Rua in áirde is a cúis dá fhreagairt dó,
Counsilear Day is e a plé ina seasamh dó
Taimse im chodladh is ná dústear mé

The impact of the famine in Kerry is dramatically highlighted in the census figures for 1841 and 1851. Almost every townland shows a marked decrease in population in the second census. Some examples from the Milltown area: In 1841 there were 797 people living in the village of Milltown; ten years later the figure was 485. The townlands of Callinafercy East and West had a combined total of exactly 800 people in 1841; in 1851 the figure had shrunk to 552. The townlands of Kilderry North and South declined from 329 to 127, and the same pattern is repeated in all the townlands of the parish of Kilcoleman—Abbeylands, Ballyoughtra, Ballymacandy, Clonmore and Knockavota.

One of the visitors to Kerry in the 1850s, in the immediate wake of the famine, was the American, Harriet Martineau. She is one of the very few writers of the period to mention the workhouse at Killarney:

There is the grand Cathedral. It is a melancholy sight, that half-developed edifice, standing on the bright sward, unused and unusable. Another great building is the workhouse, now, by the addition of wings after the famine, become indeed a very large building. It is one of the best-managed houses in Ireland, strangely and mournfully populous. The neighbourhood, thinned by death and emigration, still yields a large workhouse population in the summer, when the harvest is gathered in the fields and strangers are swarming on the lakes.

Though, in general, the workhouse was a dreaded institution and the fear of 'ending up there' was very real, none of the older residents in Callinafercy can recall anyone from the area going there. One old lady said, 'The fishing was always a great boon to the people of Callinafercy— it kept them going.'

The River Maine was not only important because of the fishing; before the coming of the railways in the mid-1800s river transport was essential for those involved in trade of any kind. A guide-book compiled in 1803 had this reference:

The river is deep enough for vessels of a hundred tons and upwards to sail to the bridge (at Castlemaine) at high water; some vessels are unloaded here on the bankside which serves as a wharf. They are generally freighted with rock salt from England, considerable quantities of which are refined in this neighbourhood; others are laden with iron-ore which is carried on horses to the iron foundry at Muckross.

In the 1830s corn was the principal export from Castlemaine, but following the building of a quay and warehouse at Callinafercy, conveniently close to the mouths of both the Maine and the Laune, trade at Castlemaine began to decline.

The flooding of the land beside the Maine (which was still happening in the fifties) seems to have been a recurring problem through the centuries. Naturally, its rise and fall was watched with the same intensity that the natives of Egypt were said to bring to bear upon the Nile, and memories of bad years lingered long in folk memory. In the late-eighteenth century, a Ralf Marshall of Callinafercy, with the assistance of a Dutch engineering company, organised the construction of river banks; the flooding continued, however, and the potato fields of the tenants were completely submerged beneath a deluge of water from time to time. A letter written in Callinafercy in the 1880s paints a sombre, if sardonic, picture of the tribulations endured:

> John Joy of Anaghdale, a most respectable man, is leading an amphibious life for the last month. His out-offices are flooded and he is driven to the side of fences to seek an unavailing protection for his cows. Timothy Clifford of Callinafercy stands in a worse plight still. He had to evacuate his place long ago. His potatoes are rotted away. His rick of hay is only kept from being swept away by means of sticks and ropes, and by the front of his house flows a stream that would float a barge.

Still, as they used to say, if it wasn't one thing it was another. In the 1880s a big fall of snow hit the Milltown area and the bad weather seemed to have lasted for about two weeks:

> There was a big fair held in Milltown a little before Christmas at that time. The people that came to the fair had to tie *sugáns* around their legs so that they would be able to walk. That same year the ice on the River Maine was so thick that the late Sir William Godfrey walked across it with his dog.

River transport was further developed with the introduction of a ferry service between Keel, on the road to Dingle, and Callinafercy, in the late-nineteenth century. At a meeting held in March 1881 it was proposed that 'a company be formed, with a capital of £1,000 in one thousand shares of one pound each, fully paid up; and that the Grand Jury be asked at the next Summer Assizes to construct the necessary slips at the quays of Keel and Callinafercy. Before the meeting ended applications had been made for over four hundred shares. The saving in carriage which the ferry introduced can be gauged from the fact that 'Keel, by way of Castlemaine, is ten miles from Killorglin, while the ferry shortens the distance to four miles.'

In common with the rest of Ireland, poverty and hardship were widespread in the Milltown area in the nineteenth century. A circular letter sent by Major Leeson-Marshall to a group of tenants in 1882 reads as follows:

Gentlemen, owing to the late harvest being so bad and taxes high, I think it right to give the following abatements on the half-year's rent to be collected on or before the 20th of next month: Twenty-five per cent on the highlands and fifteen per cent on the other townlands. Any farms, the rents of which have been permanently abated, will not be entitled to the reductions mentioned. The abatements are conditional on my rents being paid by the date stated. If not, full costs will be enforced and all allowances for money will be stopped.

Evictions and threats of eviction were commonplace. The Land League had been founded in 1879 by Charles Stewart Parnell and Michael Davitt to protect the interests of tenants and it became very active in the Milltown area in the decade between 1880 and 1890. A meeting held in Milltown at the farm of a man named Tangney, who was under threat of eviction for not paying his rent, suggests the temper of the times. Contingents came from Keel, Castlemaine, Killarney, Killorglin and Tuough, the latter headed by a Mr. Geoffrey O'Donoghue, who arrived on horseback 'wearing a green sash and rosette'. The first resolution was that 'the present land system of Ireland is destructive of the best interests of the country and we demand radical change'. The second proposed that no one should take a farm from which a tenant had been arbitrarily evicted for non-payment of any unjust rent, and the third and final one read: 'That in any settlement of the land question we demand and hereby promise, that due provision must be made for the labouring classes of this agricultural country.'

One old man told us that his grandmother had been evicted from the family homestead, one of the oldest houses in Callinafercy:

> Her name was Mag Brien. She was what they called an eleven months' tenant and at that time when someone couldn't pay their rent there were plenty of people waiting to jump in and take the place. She got a house further up the road afterwards, and most of her children emigrated to America and Australia. Years afterwards my brother asked what rent did she owe when she was evicted and he was told just one year's rent.

Opponents of the Land League in Kerry sought to belittle its objectives, with mildly satirical poems such as *The Matin' of the Land League*:

> There is not in this wide world a valley so swate,
> As that vale in whose bosom the Parnellites mate;
> Och, the last race of landlords and gents must depart
> Ere the bloom of the sparkin' shall fade from
>   my heart.
>
> Yet it was not that each man enlivened the scene
> With shamrock cockades and sashes of green;
> 'Twas not that good lashings of drink did us fill—
> Och, no, it was something more comforting still.
>
> 'Twas that bullets concealed in our bosoms were near,
> Which made every dear life of a landlord more dear;
> And we felt sure that ould Ireland would surely
>   improve,
> If we only could use all the weapons we love.
>
> Swate vale of our matin we never shall rest,
> Till we get the fine livin' and aise we love best;
> When the rint that we pay in this cold world shall aise,
> And whiskey, the craythur, be mingled in pace.

The Godfreys, like landlords elsewhere, were keenly interested in the Land League. A letter written by one of them in 1880 contained the following:

> I hear there are some people arrested at last under the Coercion Act, but Leaguing is supposed to be dying out quietly since the Land Leaguers have begun to disagree amongst themselves. There was a large meeting in Tralee on Sunday and the Killorglin band was playing in Milltown, such a horrible noise of drum and fife.

Lady Edith Gordon, sister of Major Leeson-Marshall, showed more understanding. Writing in the 1930s, and aware of the virulence of the campaign in Kerry, she remarked that some of the 'outrages' perpetrated by the Land Leaguers could be justified in the sense that very often they were 'the result of callous evictions'. It was a campaign, she observed, which eventually led to much-needed reform in the land laws and a series of Acts, from Ashbourne's to Wyndham's.

The coming of the railway was an event of great significance since it made travel easier, and remote isolated areas which had previously been largely inaccessible were now within reach. One of the most scenic railway routes in the country must surely have been that from Farranfore to Valentia via Milltown, a journey which began under the shadow of the mountains of Killarney and finished with the seascapes of Dingle Bay. The railway stations along the route were picturesque examples of Victorian architecture and ironwork at their best. That in Milltown was one of the architectural gems of the village and is still remembered for the colourful floral displays on the platform.

The first section of the line between Milltown and Killorglin was opened in 1883, and there is in existence a very old photograph showing a group of men, with horses in the background, laying another section of the line two years later. In the picture is Daniel O'Sullivan of Callinafercy who later became a milesman on the Great Southern and Western Railway.

Among the travellers on the inaugural four-mile journey from Milltown to Killorglin were one hundred boys from the Monastery School, who were treated to the free train journey by their teacher, Brother Malachy MacSweeney. It was a great event by all accounts and crowds of people gathered in the fields to witness for themselves the wondrous invention that had come to the area. Long lines of donkeys and carts assembed all along the route, filled with people who had to see to believe, and the cheers of the crowds expressed both their enthusiasm and disbelief. One old woman from Milltown refused to believe that any horse—iron or otherwise—could run without being first fed with hay or oats; she persuaded her son to take her to see the great train for herself and was apparently so mystified, and paradoxically so contented, with what she had seen that she died happily soon afterwards. The boys who went on that first free excursion to Killorglin had to make the return journey on foot but it had been a colourful and exciting day and one that they would never forget.

One of the biggest crowds ever to leave Milltown station, according to the older generation, was that which travelled to the great Cork Arts and Crafts Exhibition of 1903; many locals were encouraged to make the journey because a woman from the parish had entered a model of an Irish thatched cottage in the exhibition. Another great throng boarded the train in 1913 to attend the historic All-Ireland Final between Kerry and Louth.

Faction fighting, organised and often lethal battles with sticks and stones between rival families or clans, was a favourite diversion in the last decades of the nineteenth century. During the fights handkerchiefs were in frequent and liberal use to mop up the blood and gore from the crop of sore heads and broken limbs that were very much the order of the day, and a field in our locality, known as the handkerchief field was, we were told, 'the bloodiest field in Ireland'.

In those days there was a brass band in Milltown; it had been formed by the local curate, Father McCarthy O'Connor and it played regularly at gatherings of all kinds. In 1890, an anti-Parnell meeting was held in Castleisland. The speakers were Justin McCarthy, T.D. O'Sullivan and Thomas Sexton, who addressed the meeting from the Crown Hotel. People from all over the country travelled to Castleisland and Father O'Connor's band was there too. Not surprisingly, large numbers of Parnellites were among the crowd and they cheered so loudly for Parnell that no word could be heard from the speakers. The meeting ended in a minor brawl between the opposing factions, and the police—inevitably there was always a large police presence at such gatherings—were forced to intervene. Clashes ensued between members of the Royal Irish Constabulary and the rival groups, and one of the band's instruments, a coronet, was seized by a policeman. In retaliation, a Moriarty from Milltown grabbed a baton from an RIC man and carried it off; the self same baton was put on display in the local library—and there it remains to this day!

An amusing story from Callinafercy illustrates the length to which law-abiding citizens would go, in order not to fall foul of the law:

> The police were very particular about dog licences wan time. There was this lad and he'd be asking the rest of um to bring him home the licence from the town but they'd come home without it. A licence was a half-crown at that time. The lad that owned the dog kept him locked up for fear he'd be spotted but at long last they brought him the licence, and says he when he was giving the dog his freedom, 'You're there today, in spite of King and Queen.'

The old storyteller gave a hearty laugh at this juncture and added by way of explanation, 'The King was the law in them days and no more about it'. The underlying tension of the times surfaces in another story about the RIC: 'The lads used go round with the biddy on Biddy's night but they'd get fined if they went into a town wearing a mask. Them were troubled times and the police were afraid of strangers coming in doing harm.'

As a child I often heard stories of the days of the War of Independence. My mother, then a schoolgirl, sometimes encountered Black and Tans in their khaki uniforms as she went to and from school. In the Milltown area, one of the most remembered events was the removal of the emblem of the Crown Hotel from an exterior wall. This was a fine plasterwork model of the lion and the unicorn struggling beneath the crown, a symbol of allegiance that the locals in those republican times were not over-enamoured of. One of the men involved told me about it: 'One night myself and a crowd of the lads got a ladder and placed it up against the wall of the Crown. We hacked every piece of the lion and the crown and the unicorn to bits and there was a pile of rubble on the ground the next morning.' There was

an RIC barracks at Milltown, with a complement of three constables and a sergeant, but it ceased to function as a barracks in 1920 when they were transferred elsewhere. An attempt was then made to blow up a section of the building, and following an explosion one Sunday morning a gaping hole appeared in the front wall.

My aunt often sang a song about an ambush which took place in Castlemaine 'in the bright month of June, in the year 1921'. The Black and Tans turned up on the usual marauding expedition and were taken on by the Kerry Brigade. Casualities followed. Jack Harvey was wounded 'some place about the nose', and 'Quirke fell down beside him and never more he rose'.

> Cooney thought he'd do the dickens,
> He thought he'd kill them all.
> But when he came to Hanafins
> Sure Cooney got a ball.

The cry was then 'Reprisals! Oh, reprisals! Three houses in each village for six of our gallant lads.'

During the Civil War that followed the War of Independence, Kerry was mainly on the Republican side that refused to accept the Treaty (the Government forces were known as the Free Staters). There were many Republican fugitives in the woods about Callinafercy. One was a man who gave and received signals by flag, communicating with an associate in Killorglin. One old man, who was a child in Callinafercy then, told me about one dramatic incident in which he figured:

One time we children were taking a boat down from the quay to the *cluisin* and there was a huge ship unloading goods at Ballykissane pier at the time. That time most of the goods coming into Killorglin came by ship—if they attempted to come by road they'd surely be commandeered. We went down to have a look at the ship and the Free Staters started firing at us from Ballykissane. Father O'Sullivan was paying one of his first visits to his native place as a priest and he was with us in the boat. He had persuaded us to take him with us, and while the bullets were flying above our heads we had to lie flat in the boat. I remember Kathy was then a child. She was dressed in a furry white coat that had come in a parcel from America and she was running along the strand. She had to run round the wall into the old little house. 'Twas a miracle she wasn't shot with all the firing that was going on. That time you couldn't walk along the cliff road but the Staters would start firing at you from across the river in Ballykissane. I remember to see the lads (Republicans) crawling on their knees up the road.

My aunt said that 'the ould people were great people to put up with all that racket and danger and still carry on with their work'.

Another Milltown woman, Mrs. Teahan, who was an active member of Cumann na mBan (the woman's arm of the Republican movement) also had very vivid memories of the Civil War:

I was working as a housekeeper in the Dominican Priory in Tralee and I had a room in a private house across the way. We used to bring messages to the lads. Mr. Power's house was the Cumann stronghold and we'd go there to get the messages. One night there was a knock at the door and when I saw the trench coats I knew we were done for. I ran up the street but I was caught just near Tylers' shop. Three of us were kept in Tralee jail for about a week. Some of the lads were in the cell opposite. A lad from Cahirciveen used ask us, 'Girls, would ye like a bit of currant bread?' Of course, Mr. Power sent us up baskets of buns and we passed some of them to the lads when the sentry was marching down to the other side of the small yard in front of the jail.

After some time, Mrs. Teahan was transferred to Kilmainham Jail in Dublin where her fellow prisoners included Grace Gifford, wife of James Plunkett, and Nora Connolly O'Brien, daughter of James Connolly. Mrs. Teahan vividly remembered conditions in Kilmainham:

> The food was very bad—a mug of tea with a small piece of bread and butter in the morning. The tea was like *uisce liath* that had been left boiling all night. We got soup in the middle of the day with *suilins* in it. We always got two spuds and if one of them was bad we could complain all we liked but we still had to eat the bad one. There was little or no recreation. Some of the prisoners worked in the kitchens. If someone had a book to read they considered themselves lucky; no newspapers were allowed but there was a big exercise yard and that was important.

Mrs. Teahan had special memories of the beautiful and talented Grace Gifford: 'Grace was a very good artist and one of the things I will always remember is the lovely picture of Our Lady she painted. We girls often stood before it and said our prayers. I often wondered what happened to the lovely picture afterwards'.

When Mrs. Teahan finally left Kilmainham she took with her a copybook bearing the signatures of all her companions, not only those of Nora Connolly O'Brien and Grace Gifford but the many other now forgotten heroines, all of whom shared a strong commitment to their own particular vision of the Ireland of the future.

During those Civil War years life at the big houses around was just as traumatic. Lady Edith Gordon described many raids on her home at Ard na Sidhe at Caragh Lake. Callinafercy was less troubled. On one occasion a single horse was taken, and another time a pony and trap were requisitioned to transport a man, wounded in an ambush on the Free State barracks in Killorglin, to the quayside, from where he was ferried across the River Maine to the relative safety of the distant shore; the pony and trap were subsequently returned to Major Leeson-Marshall.

Emigration was always a stark reality of life for the whole neighbourhood, and there was scarcely a family that did not have a son or daughter in New York or Boston.

A Milltown man who had worked as a gardener in a country house in the vicinity, owned by Seybourne May—wages five shillings a week and a good dinner every day—decided to emigrate in the early twenties and make a new life for himself in America. His memories of the voyage centred around a head of cabbage:

> I travelled from Milltown railway station to Queenstown. I then went from there to America on board a huge ship called the *Sethia*. We were at least nine or ten days at sea and some people suffered from seasickness. A fellow from Callinafercy had a bag of cabbage he was bringing over to his relatives in America but he was forced—after a lot of argument—to throw it overboard by one of the officials. We had a right laugh over the cabbage even though we felt lonely too. A lot of the boys and girls went to work in the big houses as they had done at home but my first job was with the Great Atlantic and Pacific Tea Company. I worked in one of their stores.

The migrant's departure to the US was celebrated at the American Wake—a custom which continued until the late thirties. When my aunt Nora emigrated in 1927, another aunt who was present at her 'wake' told us about it:

> All the neighbours were there and they brought little presents. They used often give pure white linen handkerchiefs with shamrocks on them, or maybe a plain little blouse. If 'twas a man was emigrating they'd most likely give him a pair of socks. My mom and the ould

women were *olagónin* and poor Nora was very lonesome
altogether. We hadn't a lot of money but anyone that
was going to America always got a good send-off, so there
was porter for the men and wine for the women and
plenty tea and currant bread. There was people in and
out of the house all night. Then when the dawn came,
they all walked with Nora over to the station at Milltown—
a huge gang altogether. There we said our last good-bye,
and the train pulled away again, smoke puffing from the
engine. Then there was a card from Queenstown, saying
she got there all right and 'twould be another three weeks
to a month before we heard that she was after arriving
safely in America.

In spite of the underlying sadness of the occasion, the
American wake was a convivial party, with dancing, music
and song. One interesting dance called the 'brush dance'—
a favourite of my father's—was a feature of the night. The
brush was laid flat on the floor and the dance involved
a complicated series of intricate steps and movements
backwards and forwards across the handle of the brush.
When we saw my father do the brush dance in the fifties
we children thought it looked quite simple but that was
before we saw others attempt it! On one occasion, when
a few old ladies tried to follow his lead, he advised them
to stop or 'they'd be insurance cases before long'.

Naturally songs were sung, long and lonely songs in
keeping with the mood of the evening. Some of the finest
Irish folk-songs dealt with the theme of emigration,
underlining the bleak reality that the emigrant would in
all probability never see family and friends again. In these
days of swift and easy communication, it is sometimes
difficult to understand the finality usually associated with
emigration to America in those days. My aunt Nora did
return to Ireland in the sixties, almost forty years later,
but during her American wake she burst into tears during

one of the songs, saying that she would never see any of her old friends again and this indeed was the fate of the majority of emigrants.

My uncle Tim, who emigrated to America in the twenties, was luckier; he was able to return home for a short visit in the thirties; when he went back again he travelled as a steerage passenger on the luxury liner *Lancastria*. Some time later he sent home a photograph of the liner, writing that he had landed safely in Halifax (from where he made the thirty-six hour train journey to New York), that the voyage had been pleasant and that the *Lancastria* was a beautiful ship. He specially asked that the photograph be framed and so the *Lancastria* acquired pride of place on one of the whitewashed kitchen walls.

A song that was always sung at the wakes in Callinafercy was *Marshall's Flowery Vales*, written by a woman of the area before she herself emigrated to America. The phrase 'Marshall's Flowery Vales' refers to the gardens at Callinafercy:

> Far far from Erin's sainted Isle,
>   Three thousand miles away;
> There set me down with cares around,
>   To write a pensive lay;
> Those happy thoughts of bygone days;
>   Sweet memories still remain;
> When first I knew those boys so true,
>   Round Marshall's Flowery Vales
>
> For 'twas there I wrote these rugged lines,
>   With all my heart aflame.
> And 'twas there I cried with friends beside—
>   I might not come again.
> For cruel fate forced me away,
>   Across the Atlantic waves,
> Far over from my native land;
>   From Marshall's Flowery Vales.

There's not a place in Erin's Isle,
   But is revered by me.
Its lakes and fells and shining dells,
   From the centre to the sea.
There is one dear spot I dearly love,
   Untouched by winter gales;
It's a bright calm scene all robed in green,
   Round Marshall's Flowery Vales.

Hurrah, Hurrah, here goes my sail;
We'll meet; we'll meet in Drywall sweet;
Round Marshall's Flowery Vales.

Another favourite was *The Hills of Kilderry,* part of which
I quoted in Chapter 5. At wakes the last verse had an added
poignancy:

Yet wherever I wander I'll think of Kilderry,
Though the waves of the ocean between us do swell,
So I'll now bid adieu to the Kingdom of Kerry,
And charming Kilderry forever farewell.

As children we often heard stories of those emigrants
who had found fame and fortune in the states. Among the

most notable from our locality was William Hannafin, who emigrated in 1889 at the age of fourteen. He could already play the tin whistle and violin, and in America he took up the bagpipes. One day the young Kerry piper was heard playing at the Saint Leon Hotel by a guest who was so impressed that he offered to provide lessons and tuition. The man was, in fact, Patrick Tuohy, one of the most eminent Irish-American musicians of the period. On his death, Hannafin inherited his set of Taylors Union pipes, and studied further, finding many old tunes in O'Neill's celebrated *Book of Irish Melodies*. He became one of the first to actually record traditional Irish music in America.

Many emigrants, however, found the settling in process difficult. One local man, who had been sent out to fetch a jug of milk from a nearby store, found on his return that he could not identify the house where he lodged, each house being a replica of the next. Nothing daunted, he hailed one of the passers-by and asked, 'Did you see any lad with a jug in his hands coming out of wan of them doors a few minutes ago?'

At Christmas-time, the American letter, usually enclosing a few dollars, was eagerly anticipated. We regularly got letters from aunts and uncles who had emigrated in the twenties. They were invariably cheerful, rarely making reference to the loneliness and hardship endured by so many in those early years. Many of them worked long hours as domestic servants in the town houses of the rich—the first experience of all my aunts in the land of opportunity. But though life was invariably hard there was, too, a sense of challenge for those who were willing to accept it, the challenge of surviving and finding a niche in a highly competitive social system that was far removed from the lonely little roads and the plaintive curlew cries of rural Ireland.

Of course, not all emigrants went to the States. England was a natural choice and we frequently heard that everything there had been built by the Irish labourer. The English migration had its own songs, one of which was *The Youth who Strayed from Milltown:*

Last week as the newspaper tells us—
An Irishman did stray away.
He went in search of employment,
As thousands before him did stray.
He resolved to travel to England,
For labour to seek up and down.
He never denied where he came from—
In Kerry a place called Milltown.

One morn as he walked out thro' London,
He met with John Bull on his way.
And just as he passed by a corner—
He stopped and these words he did say:
'Good morning—Where are you bound for?
And when did you land on our shore?
Are you one of those Fenians
We had in the year '64?'

Says the youth: 'Do not talk of the Fenians,'
As he looked at John Bull with surprise.
'But remember the last words of Emmet,
For they were the cause of much noise—
And is it because I'm from Ireland,
That you look upon me with a frown?
And remember I'm the wrong hero . . .'
Says the young youth who strayed from Milltown.

Says John Bull: 'As a stranger you're saucy—
No doubt your expressions are meet—
But you know that we beat down the Russians,
And the Zulus we went to defeat.
We conquered what'ere came before us,
Like thunder our cannons did roar.
We made proud Napoleon surrender,
An exile on a far distant shore.'

'And why can't you stay in your country?
Like Wild Geese, you do stray away,
To America, Queensland, New Zealand—
You never tire of crossing the sea.
Why don't you be sometimes contented,
A living to make of your own?
Like thousands around you, contented,
Who never went a mile from their homes.'

Says the youth: 'We must go from our country,
Where coercion is ever our foe.
But tell me, who are the right owners—
Of the land where the dear shamrock grows?
And as long as the green flag is waving,
An Irishman won't be put down,
And bold Parnell is our leader.'
Said the youth who strayed from Milltown.

World War II or 'The Emergency' brought the black market to Kerry, when tea and sugar were available in local shops at a pound a pound. Many shopkeepers cycled to Tralee and back, a distance of seventeen miles each way, to acquire supplies, which they in turn passed on to the consumer, having further inflated the price. A rhyme which was often sung by people of my mother's generation was:

God bless de Valera and Sean McEntee;
Who gave us brown bread and the half ounce of tea.

Scores of ships were being torpedoed in the North Atlantic and large quantities of wreckage were washed up on Kerry beaches. One man remembered visiting Rossbeigh in the forties: 'Amongst the many items I found lying on the sands were a wallet containing fifty dollars, a suitcase containing sailors' clothes and a small table marked Capitaine!'

8
Christmas and other Festivals

Christmas was a very special time in rural Ireland. Early in December we always whitewashed the interior walls, varnished the doors and painted the ceilings, and, of course, cleaning the chimney for the arrival of Santa Claus was one of the most important Christmas preparations. In some areas it was customary to push a holly-bush up and down inside the chimney stack to loosen the soot. In other houses it was the practice to send a goose fluttering down the chimney, but this was a method of chimney cleaning that never found favour in Callinafercy; no harm came to the goose, let me hasten to add, and it soon shook the soot from its feathers.

At the Lighthouse we had a problem. The crane in our fireplace was embedded in the hearth and could not be removed, to scrape or wash away the soot. So my father made a *sugán* (a rope of twisted straw), which he twined around the upright of the crane and along the pivoting arm; the straw was then set alight, burning away the soot on the crane and in the chimney. Finally the two sides of the fireplace were whitewashed, and the snowy whiteness of the lime and the blackness of the chimney made a striking contrast.

Christmas would not have been Christmas without the journey to Killorglin in the donkey and cart, my mother with her long list of groceries and other essentials of the season, including the big white candles that would brighten our lives right through the twelve days of Christmas. Most of the grocers gave each of their customers a Christmas box or present—usually a barmbrack or a small cake or a bottle of wine. My grandmother used to recall the time, in the twenties and thirties, when the local shopkeeper, Maggie Shea, would present her customers with beautiful jugs full of jam; they were rarely entrusted to the children, who would inevitably have eaten the contents on the way home. In Killorglin the men would have a Christmas drink in the pub where all was good humour and joviality, and, like most children, my brother and I were sent to the barber to have our hair cut so that we would look 'a bit respectable over the Christmas'.

My mother reared turkeys for the Christmas market and during the weeks before Christmas the yard would be filled with their gobbles and squabbles. Most of them were sold to the neighbours but a few others were taken to the market in a donkey rail. The day of the market was a day of noise and haggling, bargaining and weighing, with the rails of turkeys ranged along the streets. It was common to see men and women cycling home in the evening, with the live turkey they had purchased carefully wrapped in a coarse brown bag on the carrier. Bargains were often confirmed and sealed with a quick drink in the pub, even though my mother hated drinking because 'the sherry goes to my head'.

We always spent part of a day in a nearby wood, searching for holly and greenery to decorate the house. As we travelled the woodland paths we might catch a glimpse of a rabbit or a fox, or my father would show us the set of a badger. Cutting the holly was always a delight and my father saw to it that we never took more than we needed. When we had collected a little bundle, he would tie it with a rope and carry it home on his back. The holly was placed over the pictures and round the fireplace, while the laurel was reserved for the shelves and the top of the dresser. Varieties of holly such as Silver King or Silver Queen were virtually unknown in the country at that time but there was a magnificent variegated holly growing close to the big house, and Mrs. Ruth always allowed us to cut off a few pieces. These sprigs were treated with a special kind of reverence and respect and 'going for the variegated holly' was yet another of the pleasant and nostalgic rituals associated with Christmas. It was considered unlucky to burn holly until Christmas had come to an end.

Once or twice I remember a visit to the Black Valley beyond the Gap of Dunloe. We travelled the long winding road which climbed higher and higher, surrounded on all sides by massive rock-strewn slopes and hills. When we reached the top of the mountain pass, we could see the lake gleaming in the distance and the peaks all around were usually covered in snow. The mountain streams were foaming white, swollen with recent rains, plunging down to the valley in frothing swirls of spray. Holly-trees, covered with scarlet-red berries, grew in crevices between the rocks. The sheep had been brought down from the heights to graze on the lower slopes, while the smoke curling from the chimneys of the red-roofed whitewashed houses created a fairy-tale Christmas-card picture.

At Callinafercy we rarely got snow, but when we did it was a dream come true, with all the delights of snowmen and snowballs. Hard weather usually encouraged a robin or two to fly into the kitchen, where they were offered a tasty titbit of bread or fat from the dripping-bowl. We were always making bird-tables, very crude ones indeed, but they served their purpose. The tiny jars of water and saucers of food attracted all the birds around, including the crows from the rookery, who were less than welcome since we were more interested in helping the tiny song-birds.

We were not, however, above playing games with our visitors. A rusty old pan would be propped against a stick round which was tied a piece of twine or fishing hemp. When we had placed some food on the snow in the shadow of the pan we hid behind a barrel or a tree, holding the end of the twine in our hands. Sooner or later, a bird would approach, furtively survey the area and then begin to peck at its leisure; thereupon we would tug the twine, which would cause the stick to fall over and trap the bird beneath the fallen pan. It was a game which required a lot of patience, and success was the only reward we wanted. The imprisonment was temporary and the bird was soon on its way again, unharmed but perhaps a little baffled.

It was still the custom to give the owner of the country house the present of a turkey or goose, and when my mother worked at Callinafercy in the thirties Mrs. Marshall received many such presents. In return, she would give a piece of beef or a dark, rich, plum pudding. This latter practice was continued by Mrs. Ruth and I often watched my mother collect the ingredients for the plum puddings on the great wooden table in the centre of the kitchen. She mixed the fruit and other ingredients in a massive dark-blue and white china bowl, and when the mixture was finally ready it was put into separate bowls, which were carefully tied with muslin and steamed on the Aga cooker (which had replaced the iron range). Then they were stored on top of the kitchen dresser, ready for all those who came to make a Christmas offering. The tick of the long-case clock, the delicious aroma of plum pudding, the great blue and white bowl, the little birds eating cheese or fat from enamel bowls on the window ledge outside, the howl of the dogs in the yard—these are

my pre-Christmas images of the country house kitchen.

Preparing and decorating the candles was a job usually left to us children. Tins were filled with sand or oats and covered on the outside with coloured paper, usually green or red. We stood a candle in the centre of each tin, twining a tendril of ivy around it, and camouflaged the sand or oats with sprigs of holly. Every room had its own candle and there was an extra one for the kitchen, for New Year.

We lit our candles on Christmas Eve, usually at six o'clock, the time of the Angelus, and the privilege of lighting them was always given to the youngest member of the family—me. Then the table was set and the highlight of the Christmas tea was the grand iced cake which my mother baked and decorated with such loving care. Later she drank a glass of sherry, with the usual complaint that it was 'going to my head'. My father had a glass of stout and we children enjoyed our lemonade. There would always be a great fire in the hearth, ensured by a plentiful supply of logs from the estate. Later there would be the family rosary, plus my mother's long litany of 'extras', but the Christmas rosary was said with a special kind of fervour.

One of the loveliest customs of my childhood was that of allowing the kitchen candle to burn all through the night. It was placed in a great enamel pan in the centre of the floor and anytime we woke, restless in anticipation of Santa Claus, we could see the brightness of the candlelight flickering round the kitchen walls. The candle was distinguished from the others and referred to as 'the blessed Christmas candle', since it had welcomed the Saviour's birth. This candle was retained during the year as a source of protection for the house and family.

Santa Claus brought very little in those days but we derived as much pleasure from seeing the rabbit eating cabbage or the cat chasing a ball as we might have got from more expensive toys. Sometimes, when a photographer came to the school, we had the rare treat of getting a photo taken with Santa Claus, and many of these old photos still survive. It was well into the sixties before we had our first Christmas tree. My sister bought a set of twelve fairy lights, but if one failed the others followed suit, much to our disappointment. Among the decorations on the wall was a rosy-cheeked Santa that my mother had purchased for six old pence; happily, this much-loved Santa, now almost forty years old, still graces the walls at Christmas—a constant reminder of all the warmth of my childhood Christmasses.

As in many other places, it was customary for the man of the house and the children to go for a stroll on Christmas day, while the woman of the house prepared dinner of turkey and stuffing, potatoes and sprouts, followed by the eagerly-awaited plum pudding. If anyone called in, they were given a Christmas drink and many of the older generation had a marked preference for piping hot whiskey punch. The toast was that we should all be happy and healthy twelve months hence, but one of the old women would be sure to add philosophically, 'There'll be many changes: there'll be many changes'.

The animals were given special consideration at Christmas. The hens, the dog and the cat all got an extra generous helping of food, and Bill the donkey was taken into the shed at night, where he was supplied with all the hay he could eat. We implicitly believed the story that the animals of the world were able to speak at midnight on Christmas Eve and it made our Christmas happier when we knew they were snug and warm.

Another strongly held belief was that the gates of heaven were always open during Christmas. If any member of the local community died during Christmas, their relations were comforted with words such as, 'Aren't the gates open before them?'

On St. Stephen's Day we children celebrated by going round with the wren. We took a few branches of holly, interlaced them with brightly coloured ribbons, and went from door to door singing:

> The wren, the wren, the King of all birds,
> St. Stephen's Day was caught in the furze.
> Although he was little his family was great,
> Rise up, highland laddie and give us a 'trate'

My mother explained to us that in a race between all the birds in the world to see which could fly highest, the wren emerged victorious, having cleverly tucked away inside the wing of a great eagle for much of the race. But I was never sure why he was caught in the furze or indeed of the darker side to what seemed to us a harmless custom.

One house we liked to visit when we went round with the wren was the Twiss house, because Mrs. Twiss always gave us lemonade and barmbrack.

Nobody asked the men if they were going out with the wren. Rather they asked, 'Are you goin' round with the hobby-horse at all this year?' This was a crude wooden horse which they would drape with a white sheet and take around from door to door. They would explain that they were collecting to buy oats for the poor hungry horse, and if the householder seemed reluctant to part with a shilling or two, the jaws of the horse were moved up and down, with the jocose warning that this was a very hungry horse indeed! As a child I remember seeing the frame of a wooden horse in the loft of one of the outhouses. All the money collected was later used to buy drink and food for a grand party which was held in one of the neighbourhood houses.

On New Year's Eve, my mother, who baked a fresh cake of bread each day throughout the year, had a cake in readiness to bang against the door at the stroke of midnight. This ritual was undertaken with a great deal of solemnity and seriousness, while the other members of the family blessed themselves near the lighted candle in the kitchen. The underlying idea seemed to have been to banish hunger from our land by transferring it somewhere else—in some parts the Turks were the recipients of the curse in my young days. The candle in the kitchen was replaced with a new one on New Year's Day, perhaps symbolising the dawning of a new and hopeful period in our lives.

The religious significance of Christmas was always uppermost in our minds. Mass was celebrated in the national school a week or so before Christmas and this was a pre-Christmas tradition that had long been cherished. During the Christmas period we attended all the services and admired the Christ Child in the crib, which was made entirely from twigs of holly. This spiritual awareness heightened rather than diminished our enjoyment. The summer holidays might be longer and warmer but the Christmas holidays were the most magical time of all.

Compared to Christmas the other festivals paled into insignificance. But we did go round with the 'biddy' on the Eve of St. Brigid. Our neighbour, Jer Tim, made those fine rushwork crosses that would protect house and family during the coming year, from rushes that grew near the bank of the River Maine. It was thought important that they should be pulled, not cut, then fashioned from left to right in the shape of a cross.

On St. Patrick's Day we wore green 'ganseys', with green badges and sprays of shamrock very much the order of the day. The men wore shamrock on their hats and on their peaked caps, and almost every family in the area sent a tiny box of shamrock to some relative or other in America.

During Lent, my grandmother drank black tea, and used neither salt nor butter with her potatoes. We children gave up sweets, but as we still bought them we had large supplies of bull's eyes, acid drops, toffey and lozenges with mottos, on both St. Patrick's Day and Easter Sunday, when the ban was lifted. My father ate at least three eggs on Easter Sunday morning because no eggs were eaten during Lent, my mother selling them to a local shop. Mrs. Ruth, having reminded us to get up early to see the sun dance, often presented us with small chocolate Easter eggs which were greatly appreciated.

On May Day, we brought in branches of the summer tree. In the thirties, and indeed long before then, it was believed that if people took a little milk from each of their neighbours' cows on May morning that this would enchant the supply of milk for the year, so that their churns would produce nothing but foam. So seriously was this threat taken that many people kept their cows in on that day. My mother said that in Claodach it was considered very unlucky to give away milk on May Day, because with it would go the luck of the dairy. It had also been customary to drag a rope through the farm and then twine it round one of the stalls in the cowshed; this was supposed to ensure an abundance of milk and butter for the year.

The festival of Midsummer was celebrated on St. John's Eve on 23 June. As a boy I often heard the old people declare that there would be an improvement in the fishing catch after the flood of St. John.

One of the great occasions of our year was Puck Fair in Killorglin every August. My father often took me to Puck on the carrier of his bicycle and it was a great thrill to see so many horses in one place. I was especially fascinated by the small but beautiful Connemara ponies, which mingled among the larger breeds. There were stalls everywhere, with three-card tricksters, roulette tables, women selling candy floss, travellers dancing on the streets, and high high above, on a temporary platform, King Puck himself, grazing placidly on cabbage leaves, seemingly unaware that he was the centre of the festival. My father told me that in the thirties great pots of crubeens were boiled at Puck. Also on sale was *dilisc*, a type of seaweed that was very salty and made people thirsty, much to the profit of the publicans. My father often won prizes at the bazaar, and as we made our way happily home I hung on for dear life to a holy picture or a statue or something more earthly such as a saucepan or a clock.

In those days, every child got a *féirin* or small gift of money for Puck. One crafty old lady regularly borrowed a few sixpences from my mother which she then presented to us as a *féirin*; she had no change just then, she would tell us, and of course she would pay my mother back later— but she never did. It was said, too, that early potatoes were 'all water' until Puck had come and gone.

My grandmother told us that St. Michael's Day, or Michaelmas, used to be called *Fomhar na nGéan*, or the harvest of the geese, though, alas, the Michaelmas goose did not make its appearance on Callinafercy tables. My mother reminded us, too, that it wasn't safe to pick blackberries after Michaelmas, because the fairies 'performed' on them from that time onwards. Of course we always had Michaelmas daisies in the vase for that feast-day.

Mrs. Ruth brought us a basket of apples for Halloween, and an apple was duly suspended from the ceiling for a game of snap-apple. We also placed apples in bowls of water and tried to retrieve them with our teeth, our hands behind our backs—quite a difficult thing to do and we usually ended up soaking wet. My mother served colcannon, a traditional Irish dish of boiled potatoes and cooked cabbage which were mashed together; it had also been served in Callinafercy when she was cook to the Marshalls. As our neighbour Jack told ghost stories all year round, ghosts at Halloween were not considered to be anything special or extraordinary.

Then Christmas again. Blazing fires in the hearth, big white candles in the windows, bright green holly on the walls, and a pervasive, almost tangible feeling of togetherness all round.

9
Custom and Belief

The older generation had sayings to suit every occasion. There was a philosophical attitude to life in general, in particular to poverty, and this was reflected in sayings such as 'It is better to be born lucky than to be born with a silver spoon in your mouth'. 'Yellow silks on Julia and patches on her father' was another favourite of the twenties and thirties. Poor people were often forced to take 'the last resort', while double-dealing was discouraged by the warning, 'People who lay traps are often caught by their own bait'. My mother loved to remind us that 'When all fruit fails then welcome haw', while my father was chided for his impatience with 'Patience and perseverance got a wife for his reverence' and 'A watched kettle never boils'. As children we were constantly reminded if we ever grumbled about our lot that 'You'll never miss the water till the well runs dry!'

Newcomers to an neighbourhood were viewed with suspicion if they seemed too agreeable and pleasant: 'Too sweet by far to be wholesome' would be the verdict, while unwelcome visitors were dismissed with 'He comes without asking, like the bad weather'. My grandmother frequently said she was 'dead from the tay and dead without it', while everyone knew how to count magpies, even if our area seems to have had a slightly different version from that generally accepted:

> One for bad luck,
> Two for good luck,
> Three for a wedding,
> Four for a wake,
> Five for silver,
> Six for gold,
> Seven for a story that never was told

My mother often reminded us of a saying in common usage in her day. At the time old and diseased cattle were sent to the slaughter-house at Roscrea. So whenever anyone became extremely ill, some wag would be sure to remark, 'She's fit for Roscrea', meaning she was at death's door.

A phrase peculiar to the Milltown area in the forties was *Mo Choda Thu*. Though St. Coleman was the patron of Milltown, St. Carthage Mac Choda was the patron of nearby Castlemaine. According to local tradition he was born in Castlemaine in 564 AD and was known locally as Mochoda. When still a young man he tended his father's sheep on the slopes of dark Slieve Mish, but hearing the voices of the monks in the Abbey of Killagha he was inspired to leave the hillside and devote his life to the service of God. The phrase *Mo Choda Thu* was always used in an admiring way as an expression of praise. Thus when a player scored a goal or someone won a decisive trick in a game of cards, someone was sure to say, '*Mo Choda Thu*'.

Superstitious belief was deeply entrenched in rural Ireland, and there was a rich heritage of folk belief related to every aspect of life and living. When a neighbour came to my mother for a dozen of eggs for hatching, she invariably got thirteen, the baker's dozen, because 'If you didn't give wan egg for good luck, the eggs would be *gliogars* and you'd have no luck yourself!' The pig, the rabbit and the lone crow signified bad luck, while a cock crowing at an unusual time, especially at night, indicated a death in the family; 'I don't like to hear that fellow crowing at this hour,' a neighbour would say if he heard our cock crowing late in the evening. My grandmother hated to see a mirror broken inside the house because that implied seven years bad luck, while the same sentence awaited anyone who dared to open an umbrella indoors. A fall in a graveyard was treated with apprehension, and it was very unlucky to throw out ashes in the afternoon or 'feet water' after nightfall. Even the day one started school had a special significance. We were told that a child starting school on a Friday would never make a good scholar. If a child was particularly dense when doing his homework someone would be sure to say, 'That lad must've started of a Friday', and indeed there were many times when I felt sure I must have 'started of a Friday'. And if the clocks at the big house always told different times, that was just as well, because it was bad luck to have two clocks in the house keeping the right time. My aunt held firmly to the belief that it was unlucky to enter and leave a house by different doors. Often if she came to visit us in the summer the front door would be open, and my father would invite her to leave through the garden, then in full flower. But if she had come in through the back door, out through it she would go: 'I must go out the same door I came in.'

In Callinafercy, sparks flying out of the fire indicated that the head of the house would soon acquire a lot of money. When this happened in our house, someone would say to my father, 'Hey, Paddy, you'll be gettin' a windfall any day of these.' Much to our disappointment, however, no matter how often the sparks flew, the 'windfall' never materialised. If a knife fell on the floor, my mother would say that this meant a disappointment for one of the family, while a fallen spoon implied that we would have visitors within the next few days.

Curses were a method of retribution in vogue in the thirties and before, though they had rather gone out in my time. If rotten eggs were thrown into or buried in a neighbour's field, this would transfer some disease or bad luck to the owner. The antidote was to take the rotten eggs and burn them behind the fire; the person who had buried the eggs would subsequently get a fit of choking in the presence of the person to whom he or she wished to transfer the disease. The carcase of an old diseased hen was sometimes substituted for the rotten eggs.

Many people believed in the fairies and a colourful folk tradition grew up about these elusive, rarely seen beings. They constantly tried to lead unsuspecting mortals into danger or, with their enchanted music, lure them away from family and friends, never to be seen again. They wreaked vengeance on those who dared to interfere with their sacrosanct places of abode, the old ring-forts. Mysterious lights could be seen blazing from these forts in the blackness of the night, lights that might be the work of Jackie-the-Lantern, an audacious spirit who roamed abroad swinging a lantern by his side. Jack the storyteller, who often came to our fireside on long winter evenings, recounted in graphic detail how he had seen the mysterious Jackie night after night at various locations. We shivered and trembled as the old man told us about the strange unearthly glow, the ghostly illumination that moved across rivers and fields, its trail of light dancing behind it.

Another of his favourite stories was about a mysterious little old lady whom he often encountered along the roadway not far from our house. She always walked in front of him and one night his curiosity got the better of him. 'I drew a kick at her,' he would explain seriously, 'and what do ye think, lads, but didn't my shoe go right through her!'

It was considered extremely foolish to interfere with a fort. No farmer would plough one up, no housewife would spread clothes on the bushes around it, and we were warned that it was unwise to play round its walls—an injunction we didn't always heed. It was considered unlucky, too, to interfere with fairy pathways, recognisable because of the profusion of primroses, cowslips and other wild flowers that blossomed along these tracks. Occasionally, a foolhardy farmer would build an animal shelter right in the centre of the pathway but he invariably suffered the consequences, either through prolonged illness or through the inexplicable and unexpected death of his livestock.

People had to be very careful not to build their houses too close to the site of a fort, as they might find they were trespassing on fairy land. There was the salutary tale of a man who was building his house near a fort when suddenly a whirlwind blew up and a stranger appeared before him, advising him to knock the house down because there would never be luck in it. The man ignored the stranger's warning and built the house. On the very first night it was occupied, when the people of the house were in bed, they heard tongs fixing the fire and the sound of cups and saucers being placed on the table. Next morning they thought they would find the kitchen in complete disarray but everything was back in its place. The same disturbance happened night after night until finally the people were forced to leave the place altogether.

The fairies had also invaded a fine period house in the area belonging to the Myles family, which was known as the 'haunted house of Callinafercy'. It has long since gone but stories about it are still alive in folk memory:

> Marshall wouldn't allow anyone to cut the trees in his wood in the twenties, but the men used to cut young ash saplings that grew along the ditches. These were used as 'quins' for ploughing and they were left to season in a safe place where no one would find them. A lad that was staying at Myles's house had the quins under his bed but when he was going to bed one night, didn't he find them all stacked up inside the bedroom door. As he couldn't get into his own bedroom, he decided to sleep in another, but in the middle of the night weren't all the quins thrown up on top of him! 'Twas the joeys (the fairies) that were play actin', for they were ever known to be in that ould house.

This same house had its resident ghost, a strange ethereal woman who was regularly seen combing her hair by the fireside. People who chanced to descend the stone steps into the kitchen were sure to see her, a melancholy listless expression on her face, while her yellowing hand moved the comb through her long hair with vapid regularity. Was she a banshee? Hair combing was one of their characteristics. At Callinafercy House, built by Anne Williams in 1841,

the fairies were apparently of an agricultural turn of mind.
Bob Knightly told us this story:

> 'Twas generally horse-powered machinery that was in use
> in them times (the twenties and earlier) but they had
> a threshing-machine at the house. A few nights when it
> was standing idle in the yard, the fairies took out the
> pin and set the thing in motion. It would noise away
> for a while, with not a living Christian in sight, and then
> 'twould stop again just as suddenly as it started up.

Callinafercy House and lands, which included a cluster
of houses that were much older than the main building,
were bought by Justin McCarthy in 1910. His son—also
Justin—remembers that stories of ghosts and fairies were
commonplace at Callinafercy House in the 1940s, when
neighbours dropped in to hear news of the war on the
wireless.

The fairies made occasional forays out of the forts where
they lived. The fairies of Callinafercy loved their games of
football, which they always played in our field. We were
told that our grand-uncle was the first to witness one of
these extraordinary matches in the twenties:

> Mike Sullivan was out for a late-night stroll with one
> of the neighbours and when he had said good-night to
> his friend, he saw the little men playing their game inside
> the field. It was a very bright night and he saw the players
> clearly. He got an awful fright, the poor man. He was
> never in the better of it, for he died not long afterwards.
> A lot of other people saw the fairies playing there too.

At night we children often strained our ears, in the hope
that we might hear the thud of a fairy boot against the
football or the cheers of a fairy throng when their team
had scored, but despite our best efforts no such sounds
were ever heard by us. It was also suspected, from the
evidence of potato pots left lying around, that fairy women

sometimes came and took potatoes from adjoining fields, but when they had vanished into the fort once more, the farmer would find that no potatoes were missing.

Enchanted hares were often associated with the fairy forts of Kerry. The fairy hares of Callinafercy were particularly active and often plagued local farmers by stealing milk from their cows:

> One time a farmer became suspicious that someone was milking his cow every night. He decided to stay up all night but the only thing he saw coming out of the shed was a hare. Anyway, he fired a shot at it, and later on didn't he find splashes of blood and milk on the ground. Then he realised how 'twas the fairy hare had been stealing his milk.

The fairies also came into houses. If a kitchen was not brushed at night, for instance, they would take the person who neglected to do so. This was often the reason given for the unexplained disappearance of someone. And many were the tales of people who strayed unwittingly into a fairy fort at night and saw there friends and neighbours they had thought long dead. It was also unlucky to leave anything on chairs, because the visiting fairies might need to sit down and rest awhile. If, however, fairies were carousing in a house at night, mass could be said and they would disappear.

As if the fairies and Jackie-the-Lanterns were not enough to deter mortals from strolling out after dark, there was the additional threat of the *Madra Ciar Dubh* and the Pooka. The black dog of Callinafercy was well known to us all:

> The old people were very honest and they never made things up. They believed firmly in the big black dog, and they believed he used come out near this hawthorn tree or at other times near this gullet in the road. They'd carry a hazel stick for protection against him.

The specific reference to the hawthorn tree is interesting; it has special significance in fairy lore all over Kerry.

The Pooka was a mischievous spirit who delighted in creating havoc at every opportunity, both on land and on sea. He entered the sea after Michaelmas and made life a misery for the men on the ocean wave. A neighbour of ours disliked going for a stroll in the dark because she 'was frightened in dread of the pookies'. The 'boody man' was yet another spirit who brought terrible retribution on 'bold bad-mannered children'.

Perhaps the apparition we most dreaded was the headless coachman who figures prominently in folk tales from every part of Kerry. This sinister harbinger of death, one which had happened or was about to happen, was accompanied by the rhythmic pounding of the hoofbeats of his horses and the rattle of carriage wheels over the stony roads.

A place associated with ghosts was the *cileen* field. There was a *cileen* near the haunted house of Callinafercy, which may have accounted for its reputation, since people regarded such places with superstitious fear. The word *cileen*, literally a small church, came to mean a small graveyard. Babies who had not been baptised were buried there, 'years and years ago' my mother told us, because the people in bygone days believed it was not right to bury such babies in a churchyard. Large irregular slabs or stones were placed over the graves and these could still be seen in our own time. A sailor whose body had been washed in by the tide was also buried nearby.

Travelling at night was hazardous and those who did not wish to encounter the spirits of the dead, or something worse, were advised to take a hazel stick with them—the hazel served as a charm that kept restless spirits and malevolent fairies at a safe distance.

'A good laugh and a long sleep—the two best cures in the doctor's book' was a popular saying at a time when many ailments and disorders were treated at home. Most members of the older generation had an inherent dislike of 'doctors' medicine' and even when they did go to the doctor they retained their scepticism; my grandmother told us that she was very fond of throwing bottles of medicine—unopened—into the River Laune just outside her cottage.

Many of the home cures were based on common sense. When we got stung with nettles we rubbed dock leaves on the area. Raw onion or a portion of a bluebag, used for whitening clothes, was the remedy for a bee sting, while that for a wasp was vinegar. Coins were believed to reduce swellings and I often had an old penny placed against my forehead when I had accidentally bumped into something. Minor sprains were treated by bathing in pickled water or by keeping the affected area under cold water for some time. Indigestion could be relieved by eating a raw potato, chewing nettles or by drinking bread soda dissolved in water, while my grandmother believed that sore eyes were cured by the application of cold tea, which did indeed contain helpful tannic acid.

Other cures were based on ancient belief. Whooping cough had been cured in the thirties by cutting the tops of green furze, boiling them and squeezing the water out; a piece of candy was mixed with the dried furze and the child would be given a spoon before each meal. If a child was unlucky enough to develop the croup in the thirties, a mixture of sugar, salt and butter was prepared; this revolting mixture would invariably cause the child to vomit, which was a necessary first step in any recovery process. Ivy leaves, particularly those plucked near a stream or from the face of a cliff, were used for curing sores on the head. But what is one to make of the suggested cure for measles which prevailed until the thirties? 'If a child had measles, he was taken into the pigs' house and his mother very often pretended to throw him to the pigs. The child would scream hysterically but the shock would cure the measles for good.'

The application of wort weed was one remedy for warts while another, which my mother remembered from her schooldays, involved finding a rock with a hole containing water. The wart was bathed in this on seven consecutive days, the patient blessing himself at each visit. The cure for a whitlow, again my mother's belief, was to break an egg, remove the white and massage it against the part.

A sore throat could be cured by placing boiled potatoes in a stocking and wearing it about the neck, while goose grease was not only liberally applied to the axles and wheels of carts—it was also used to relieve pains in the legs. According to my grandmother, an old remedy for rheumatism was to gather seaweed and boil it; when the mixture was cold, the seaweed was removed and the patient bathed his hands or feet in the water. The yoke of an egg, beaten stiff with whiskey and sugar, was a favourite remedy for a pain in the stomach, while a persistent cough could be cured by boiling carrigeen moss, straining it and taking it with sugar.

As a child I often heard the neighbours talk about the cholic—a searing and debilitating pain which principally affected the stomach. Apparently there was no cure for this and many sufferers were known to roll around on the ground in the centre of an open field to alleviate their distress. Another, more desperate, remedy was to heat the cover of a pot oven until it became red hot; the heated cover was then applied near the pain. For anyone suffering from yellow jaundice, a branch of palm which had been blessed at the Palm Sunday ceremonies would be burned with a specially selected blessed candle; the ashes were mixed into the patient's drink which, when drunk, effected a speedy cure. A pain known in Kerry as 'gravel' pain was cured by eating part or all of the gizzard of a hen, while a pain in the side could be cured by applying the blood of a chicken which had been killed on St. Martin's Day and preserved on a woollen cloth.

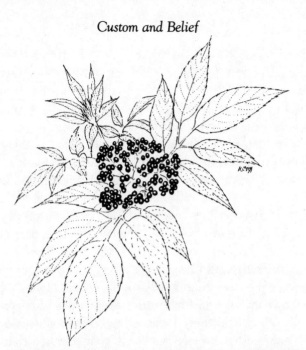

Mrs. Ruth of Callinafercy could be seen strolling through the laneways and fields each year, her basket suspended from her arm. This rushwork basket was filled with elder flowers and later elderberries. They were carefully cooked and distilled to produce a sweet-tasting wine which was both an effective antidote and cure for colds and flu.

Plants were often used in the preparation of medicines. Some were known only by their Irish names. *Slanlus* was the name given to the narrow-leaved plantain or *plantago laceolata*, the leaves of which were used, like ivy leaves, to cure sores on the head. The wild flag iris, known to us as *elestrum*, in other areas as *feliestram*, was used as a cure for toothache. In many parts of Kerry the common dandelion was known as *caisearbhan*, and it was customary in the thirties for families to pluck baskets of *caisearbhan*, which was then used to supplement other foodstuffs given to animals. *Creamh* was the name given to wild garlic, which was sometimes used as a cure for black quarters or black leg disease in animals.

There is no doubt but that some of the old remedies contained a great deal of common sense. One old neighbour of ours firmly believed that poteen improved the circulation of the blood; she advocated rubbing it on the skin but no doubt the odd drop found its way to her lips.

It must be remembered, of course, that in those days of slow and difficult transport, with no phones, the home cure was often the only one available. By the time I entered the world, however, all had changed and doctors were already indispensable members of the community. The doctors in Milltown were the Sheehans—Eamonn and his wife Anne. Dr. Eamonn's father had also been a doctor and, despite my grandmother's reservations about bottles, they were all very highly regarded. When I was a baby I suffered from eczema for a short time and a blue ointment was prescribed. So there I was, covered with blue ointment, while I supped from my bottle of goat's milk—that being the second part of the prescription.

In the olden days, if, for any reason, the home-made cure was ineffective there was always the holy well, which was never known to fail. The people believed implicitly in their power—and they had a wealth to choose from in Kerry.

My mother often visited the most famous of them, that dedicated to St Craobh-Dearg, at Shrone near Rathmore, beneath the twin peaks of Da Chich Danann (the Paps). My mother told us that the Paps represented the breasts of the goddess Dana, and that the Dananns, more widely known today as the *Tuatha Dé Danann*, were her followers, There are those in the area who claim that the well is the site of the oldest uninterrupted religious practices in Western Europe; almost four thousand years ago druids used the well, principally for immersion purposes, in rites to honour the goddess. About two thousand years before Christ these early settlers built the circle of stones and monuments close to the well. The *Tuatha Dé Danann* magically disappeared beneath the earth around the site of the well when their old religion was swept away by the advance of Christianity. Dana's shrine became the well of St. Craobh-Dearg.

A very old story from Claodach—a favourite of my mother's—told how a bull was stolen from the saint by a robber from Claodach. It was taken over the mountains, but the miraculous powers of the saint caused the footprints of the stolen bull to be firmly imprinted on the track leading away from the well. The robber was soon discovered and the bull brought back. Generations later, pilgrims to the well believed they could still see the bull's hoofprints.

May Day, which coincides with the druidic festival of *Bealtaine*, which was christianised in Ireland and dedicated to the Virgin Mary, was selected as the day for the annual pilgrimage to *Cathair Craobh Dhearg* or 'the city', as it was always known. Huge crowds went to the well and everyone brought home a bottle of holy water—the first bucket of water taken from the well that morning being specially prized. The rounds were made with great devotion and piety, while animals, particularly cattle, which suffered from some disease were driven into a fort near the well where they remained overnight, their owners hoping for a speedy and effective cure of their ailments. Kingcups and buttercups growing in the vicinity of the well were taken home to serve as charms to guarantee an abundant supply of dairy produce during the year. If these flowers were placed in a circle round the well, this would prevent the casting of spells and curses.

St. Gobnait, associated in many stories with honey bees and wild deer, was a sister of St. Craobh Dearg, and there is a well dedicated to her near Ballyvourney. The annual pilgrimage to this well takes place at Whitsuntide. My grandparents are buried within the old chapel walls, and once when we visited the well my mother showed us the sculptured head of the *gadai dubh*, the black robber who had stolen the bull of St Craobh Dearg. Embedded in one of the walls was a black leaden ball which people said held a great cure for cattle; they would rub their handkerchiefs to it and these would be rubbed against the affected area of the animal when they got home. Several times over-zealous pilgrims had actually stolen the miraculous ball and that was why St. Gobnait had embedded it in the walls of the church. Around the well, as a thanksgiving for cures, pilgrims had left old cups, bottles and pieces of cloth as well as rosary beads and medals.

St. Craobh Dearg and St. Gobnait had a sister—St. Lattern of Cullen—perhaps the least well known of the three, whose well was visited annually on the Sunday nearest to the twenty-fifth of July. An old folk-tale recounts the story of St. Lattern and the blacksmith:

> St. Lattern lived at Cullen and she used to go into the forge to get a coal (or *griosach*) to start her fire. She always carried the coal away in her apron. One fine morning the smith, admiring the saint's figure, said, 'You've a lovely pair of legs'. Flattered by this compliment, St. Lattern stopped for a moment and the coal burned a hole in her apron. She knew then that she had committed the sin of pride—so in a fury she put a curse on the forge. From that day the bellows ceased to blow and the sound of the blacksmith's hammer was never heard again in the village.

A sacred fish, particularly a trout, was said to dwell in most holy wells, and the well of *Tobar na Bhfion*, the Well of the Wine, which was near Cordal, Castleisland, was no exception. Any pilgrim who managed to catch a glimpse of the fish was immediately cured. Not far from the well was Cordal House, owned by the Twiss Family, agents for Lord Ventry. At one time the sacred trout was removed from the well and the water at Cordal House, which came from Tobar na Bhfion, refused to boil until the trout was returned to its rightful place.

There were even more disastrous consequences in another case where the fish in a holy well was disturbed. The eldest son of a landed family, variously named as Stanley or Crosbie, set his dog after 'the green spotted trout' in the holy well at Ballyheigue. The dog caught and savaged the trout—but both dog and master immediately went insane following the incident. Worse was to follow: When the culprit died, there was such a pervasive and intolerable stench from his body that workmen were often forced to abandon their work in neighbouring fields. This holy well is not directly named in the story, but it is probably Our Lady's Well, Ballyheigue, another favourite with Callinafercy and Milltown people.

Indeed, any form of disrespect at a holy well brought dire consequences. The story is told of a man who spat into the holy well of St. Senan's at Ballydonoghue. Immediately he felt that a rat was running up one leg of his trousers and down the other, continuing thus, backwards and forwards until he was forced to undress. It was, however, only his imagination; there was no rat in reality. But the delusion was taken to be a punishment for his lack of respect.

Wether's Well at Ardfert was the favourite of my Callinafercy grandmother, and in her young days she travelled there every June, usually round the feast of St. John. Sometimes she walked; sometimes a group of neighbours would take a donkey and cart. The origin of its name is explained thus:

In the bad penal times, when the priests were being hunted to death like wild beasts, it happened that a mass was being said before the old altar by the well. There were look-out men set up on the ridges above the well. Just before the elevation, there was a cry, 'The bloodhounds.' and in another minute the hounds came leaping down the slope towards the altar, their red tongues hanging out between their teeth ... and there were the soldiers rising over the ridge behind them. Now when the dogs were drawing close, up out of the well there leapt three wethers, and these set scampering off towards the north. The dogs were soon making grabs at their woolly sterns, and behind the dogs galloped the soldiers and the justices of the peace (quare justices), and such a hunt Finn MacCumhail never made—five miles to Ath Caoraig, where on a sudden the wethers disappeared into the ground, like rabbits into their holes. Only when the justices and sheriffs and soldiers came up to where the dogs were sniffing round, there was no hole to be seen.

St. Brendan the Navigator was baptised at Wether's Well, and perhaps a more plausible explanation of the name is that 'on the day of St. Brendan's baptism there, three wethers were presented to him by a holy man named Airde, who lived in the district and to whom the birth of the saint was foretold.'

St. Coleman of Milltown had no holy well dedicated to him but there was one to St. Carthage MacChoda, and rounds were performed there as late as 1948. This well was situated close to the banks of the River Maine, *Abha na Mainge*, and the pilgrim was required to walk around it before taking back some water to a holy stone, which stood on a footpath on the road from Castlemaine to Kiltallagh. The pilgrim then circled the stone and the water from the well was applied to the eyes with a piece of cloth, water from St. Carthage's Well being particularly efficacious in restoring or improving the eyesight. On a whitethorn bush growing on the ditch close to the road were little cloths which had been used by pilgrims when dabbing the water into their eyes. It was part of the ritual that the cloths should be left behind. This story was told about the holy stone of St. Carthage in the 1940s:

There was a parson lived there, Parson Murphy. He was a good man, liberal and charitable, but he was always ridiculing the rounds. He had the stone taken up and removed to his own house, the Rectory, but the stone was back in its original place the very next morning, and looked as if no one had put a hand to it. The ground around was undisturbed. So the parson came to the conclusion that it was some of the fellows of the locality that brought it down and he said they wouldn't bring it again. So he had the stone dug up a second time and he locked it in a room. ' 'Twill stop them now,' says he ... But the following morning the stone was back on the footpath, after all the locking. The parson didn't take it anymore and 'tis there today and will be forever.

Curiously the rounds at the well of St. Carthage Mac Choda in Castlemaine were associated with no particular feast day and so could be performed anytime.

The visit to the holy well was one of the most colourful expressions of a deep and gentle faith, and happily pilgrimages to holy wells such as those of St. Craobh Dearg at 'The City' and St. Gobnait at Ballyvourney continue to this day. They are a highly significant part of the folk culture of Kerry, in both a social and religious context.

10
Sad Days, Happy Days

Death was a time of sadness and lamentation. In Kerry, dogs baying or cocks crowing at unusual times were considered to be omens of death. But there were many other portents which enabled the knowledgeable to predict the worst—an inexplicable rap at the door, a tapping or hammering on the walls, strange unearthly music in the sick-room, a cabbage plant growing lone and forlorn in the centre of a field, a picture falling off the wall, horses (sold for some time) returning to their old owner's home, and a moth circling about the head at night.

In rural Ireland the dead person was always 'waked', sometimes for a few days. All the neighbours gathered in, to condole and reminisce, and prayers, including five decades of the rosary and the litany, were recited. Eating and drinking formed an indispensable part of the ceremonies because the deceased had to be given a 'good send-off'.

A certain ceremonial was attached to a wake. Those entering the house where it was taking place were required to say, 'The Lord have mercy on the dead.' In many parts of Kerry it was the custom to have thirteen candles in thirteen candlesticks on a table at the side of the dead person, representing Our Lord and the twelve apostles; one candle, the Judas candle, was left unlighted. The candlesticks were usually given by neighbours and the tradition was that they were returned to their owners afterwards. Up to the thirties, it had been the custom to distribute clay pipes and tobacco to those who came to the wake; they were given both to smokers and non-smokers and, since a refusal would signify lack of respect for the dead, it was incumbent on everyone to take at least one symbolic puff. Snuff was also distributed at wakes, much to my grandmother's delight. For some reason it was considered unlucky to stand or sit between two doors at a wake.

One question that never had to be asked at a wake was what time the death had occurred; the clock was stopped at the moment of death.

Wake games were popular in many parts of the country but they apparently never found favour in Callinafercy:

> There was never any carryin' on of any sort at a wake, for the dead person was honoured. Some of the people didn't like to go home alone after a wake. It was the custom in these parts in the old days for the priest to come to meet the funeral.

My sister vividly remembers one wake from her childhood days. An old man had died and his sister came from her own house with a large suitcase, presumably filled with clean linen and other essentials. 'When we seen her coming with the suitcase,' remarked one of the wags later, 'we wondered was it hittin' for America she was in the height of the bother?' My sister and a friend of hers succumbed to a fit of the giggles during the course of the wake, whereupon the lady with the suitcase warned them that if they didn't desist, the old man would rise up from the bed and waylay them on the road one dark night. The warning made a deep impression; for the next few days they were genuinely afraid that they might encounter the spirit of the dead man on some lonely stretch of road.

Then there was the humorous, if somewhat poignant, tale of the Callinafercy man who died about the time motor cars made their first appearance in the area. His greatest wish during his last days on this earth was that someone would hire him a motor car to take him to heaven.

Preparations for the funeral were likewise subject to ancient custom. One rule was that no person should go singly to purchase things for a funeral; that was considered very unlucky. This edict particularly applied to the coffin; 'Two or three persons must be at the purchase of that, or it would be absolutely fatal.' Certain procedures were also laid down for attendance at a funeral, and as it moved away from the house, some close relative of the person who had died was expected to remain behind. The number of mourners must never be counted; people who did so would be counting those for their own funeral. And a mourner should never visit a sick person when coming from the cemetery. In the fifties, crape (a black fabric) was worn around the men's arms, while pieces of white linen were worn, sash-like, by the priests in attendance. Keening women were no longer a feature of ceremonies then but as children we heard stories of 'the old times' when women would 'be wailing and *olagóning* all night long'.

In olden days coffins were taken to the graveyard by horse and cart but many of the older men would insist on mounting them on their shoulders and taking them all the way to the grave. The men of Callinafercy would take a coffin on their shoulders along the strand, on their way to the graveyard in Killorglin, but this practice was only a memory when I was a child. Graves were not opened on a Good Friday or on a Monday, except when a sod had been dug the previous day. Coffins were never taken in over the walls of a graveyard (usually beside a ruined ivy-clad abbey or church, devastated in Cromwellian times). Relatives were not allowed to place the last sod on the grave of the dead person, but it was once the custom, when the father of a young family died, that the children who were old enough would jump across the grave three times, which must have been a harrowing experience. Rain was taken as a good omen at a funeral: 'Happy the corpse the rain falls on.'

Walking towards an oncoming funeral was frowned upon; anyone who happened on a funeral coming towards him had to turn round, take three steps in the direction of the cortège and make the sign of the cross. A funeral met at night signified the death of a friend far away.

After the funeral it was customary in the Callinafercy area to give away, if not the entire wardrobe of clothes, at least one suit or dress, to a relative or friend of the the dead person. This happened when my grandmother died in 1959, and when my father died his best suit was given to his brother, my uncle Donal. Those who received the clothes were expected to wear them at least three times to mass, and one of these masses should, according to tradition, be offered for the soul of the deceased. Relatives who refused to part with some of the clothes of the dead person were said to suffer from dreams and horrors, many of them associated with the dead. Mourning was taken seriously; when my father died in the sixties, my mother wore black for a year afterwards and we were not allowed to listen to the radio for a few months, except for news.

No account of death in Ireland would be complete without mentioning the banshee (*bean sídhe* in Irish), literally the fairy woman, whose wailing cry was to be heard upon the death of members of certain families. Her hauntingly high-pitched cry aroused terror and dread, not only among those who heard it but also those who had had it described to them in minute and graphic detail. I often heard about it from my grandmother, as she and the women of her generation firmly believed in her existence. A strange luminous sphere, hanging in the blackness of the midnight sky, was sometimes associated with the lament or *caoineadh* of the *bean sídhe*.

But life in the country was not all funerals and lamentations. In those days before television and radio, neighbours travelled to a selected house for an evening of conversation and music. In the Irish phrase people were *ag bothántaíocht* (which can be loosely translated as rambling), and the houses were sometimes referred to as 'rambling houses'. Unaccompanied *sean nós* (Irish songs sung in a traditional way) as well as the recitation of verse were part of the evening's entertainment, while music was provided by the violin, the melodeon and the *bodhrán*, an ancient Irish musical instrument made from goatskin stretched over a wooden frame. Dancing was very popular and indeed there had been a dancing-school in Callinafercy in the twenties, at Hannafin's house. Reels, jigs, hornpipes and traditional sets, as well as the ever-popular 'brush dance', were all performed with verve, the shadows of the dancers silhouetted on the walls by the flames flickering in the hearth. One old neighbour of ours remembered those evenings well:

> They had country dances in the houses at that time, for the old people were nice step-dancers. The floors were all earthen floors, of course, but they'd have a big flag in front of the fire for the dancers.

Sometimes the highlight of such evenings was a story told by the local *seanchaí* (storyteller). There was at least one in every area and he had a vast fund of stories, old and new. Seamus Ó Maille was the most famous *seanchaí* in Callinafercy and it was said that he could tell very long stories about the Fianna in Irish, recounting the exploits of these legendary pre-historic heroes as if they had happened yesterday. Part of the *seanchaí's* art was to enlarge and enrich his story with local references and witticisms, and pace and timing were all-important. Audience reaction was an essential part of the performance.

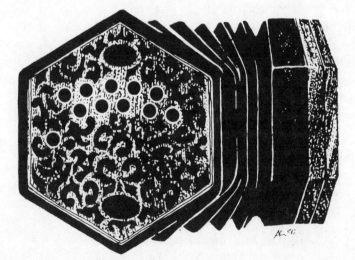

Another winter-time activity was card-playing, especially near Christmas when games would be organised with a turkey as the prize. There were usually eight players to each table or game and each player paid a small fee (about two shillings) to join. These sessions were happy social occasions and half way through the night tea was served with (if it happened to be in our house) great chunks of my mother's home-made apple pie and currant bread smothered in fresh creamy butter. Children of the competitors were welcomed and they had their own private amusements and games.

As the days grew warmer and the evenings longer, the cross-roads dance was the favourite meeting-place for young and old. Where the country by-roads crossed, not far from the local school, a raised platform was erected by the side of the road under the shade of the birch-trees. Young and old gathered to dance and listen, and the music makers came in great numbers; in those days music was a way of life and the people of the locality had inherited a great tradition.

The songs which were sung at such social gatherings were often composed by local poets and songsters. As we lived near the coast and fishing was a major occupation, many of the songs were associated with the river, the wind and the tide. One such song, *The Dawning of the Day*, was sung to the air of an old Fenian ballad; the words had been changed to recount how the fishermen had outwitted an over-zealous water bailiff:

On the seventeenth of January,
    When the snow was on the ground.
Our boats we did get ready,
    And for fishing we were bound.
We fished from Knightly's Island,
    And from that down to the quay,
We had our boats in action,
    At the Dawning of the Day.

When on comes Christy Power,
    With a map all in his hand,
And calling to the fishermen,
    To surround him on the strand.
Then up stands brave Jack Murphy,
    The bravest man of all,
'You want to fool us like before,
    At the Dawning of the Day.'

The bailiff's boat got badly broke,
    She drew too near the strand,
And meeting there with young Langford,
    He would not let her land;
Bassy in the garden—
    He gave a loud hurray,
When he saw the boats at Maithreach
    At the Dawning of the Day.

On comes Batt Moriarty,
    Saying a bailiff I will make.
But if a jolly scalcrow,
    Happened to pass the way,
Another man was missing,
    At the Dawning of the Day.

The dawn of day has passed and gone,
    And we'll row the Laune again.
And nothing broke poor Power's heart,
    But the fishermen from the Maine.

It may not have been classic verse but the glorification of
a well-known local event delighted its audiences.

The regatta was another Kerry tradition. My father was
a member of many crews and took part in regattas at the
Store, Callinafercy and Cromane. The crews rowed in
ordinary fishing boats which were known locally as
'bankers'. The keen sense of rivalry between the various
townlands meant that the crews took the strenuous physical

exertion in their stride. This proud tradition was maintained in 1972, when the Callinafercy seine boat crew outstripped ten rival crews to capture the Murphy Cup at the prestigious Valentia Island regatta.

Travelling circus shows visited towns and villages all over Kerry, always arriving in a procession of brightly painted wagons, drawn by gaily decorated horses with plumes on their heads. The arrival of the first circus in the village in Milltown, in the year 1904, is now part of local folklore. The matinee performance was scheduled to start at three o'clock but minutes before the curtain was about to go up a violent thunderstorm erupted over the town. Menacing peals of thunder rolled down across the heavens and shafts of brightness pierced the rainswept gloom. The matinee had to be cancelled and not until the storm had passed, some hours later, could rescue operations begin. The tent had to be secured again, seats replaced, and pieces of equipment, scattered here and there, collected and put back in place. Local people helped with the mopping-up operation, and in true circus tradition the night show went ahead as if nothing had happened. One of the features of the circus in those days was the local parody; one of the clowns went about during the day collecting material on local characters and events which was duly served up that evening.

The 'stations', when mass was celebrated in the house, was as much a social gathering as a religious occasion. When the service and prayers had been duly concluded and the celebrant had once again 'drowned us in holy water' (to quote my grandmother), the priests were given breakfast in the best room in the house. At the stations in our house in the mid-sixties, I remember the older women of the district vying for the privilege of cooking the priests' breakfast, while my mother wisely kept in the background. Rashers and eggs sizzled in the old black frying-pan on the fire. 'The only way to do rashers properly,' said one old woman as she prodded and turned; she would have nothing to do with 'those new-fangled cookers'. Once when the priest was leaving he jokingly asked one old woman if she had had any drink (whiskey and stout were usually served to the men). Thinking he was referring to holy water she replied, 'Faith then I had then, Father, and I'm after fillin' another bottle to put under the bed when I go home because I do get terrible frightened of the thunders.' At the spring stations, my father would ask the priest to bless the boat.

Older people remembered the stations in the old days in Callinafercy—pre-1930 that would have been. At that time there were only earthen floors, so a clean coarse bag would be put down for the priest to kneel on. The priest was often asked to bless holy pictures in those days, and in one house in Callinafercy pictures which were blessed at a station about fifty years ago are still hanging on the walls, still a source of pride to the owners.

Fair days were other great occasions. My mother remembered walking with her father from their home to Killarney, a distance of some twenty miles each way. This, her first fair, made a lasting impression on her. The streets were cluttered with donkeys and carts, squealing pigs, horses and traps, cattle, and women selling crubeens. She particularly recalled her visit to the Franciscan Friary on Martyrs' Hill; she had never seen such a big and beautiful chapel before and she thought there must be hundreds of steps leading up to its great doors. When the fair was over, there remained the long and daunting journey home. Happily a man driving a horse and cart, laden with hay, offered the walkers a lift for part of the way, and sitting aloft on a high load of hay, watching the sun set over valleys and hills, was to her the most memorable part of the day.

Many marriages in those days, even into the forties, were arranged by a matchmaker. This was a time when dowries and contractual responsibilities were matters of great significance and it needed all the skill and diplomacy of the matchmaker to bring things to a successful conclusion.

Most matches were arranged during the month of November.

A very old custom that seems to have waned in Kerry in the twenties was the buying of the wedding cloak. Most of the women at the time wore a hooded cloak and this was handed down from generation to generation, passing from mother to the first daughter of the household who got married. For the daughters who married later, it was the practice to purchase each one a cloak in the nearest town. All the mothers in the surrounding countryside gathered in the little whitewashed cottage where the bride lived, and after such discussion they set off to inspect the varied wares of every trader in town. The bride was never allowed to come on this important shopping expedition; she was considered to be too inexperienced in such matters!

Before the wedding, the bride often gave a party in her parents' house to celebrate the forthcoming event. This night was sometimes called 'the gander night'. At the time meat was rarely served at country parties or dances but on this particular night everyone got a generous helping of goose.

Weddings had their own particular set of superstitions. It was the duty of the bride's mother to see that the bride did not meet another woman on the way to the church; if this happened, bad luck was sure to follow, since the first expression of good wishes to the bride should, according to tradition, come from a man. It was believed, too, that after the ceremony the bride and groom should emerge from the church through different doors.

The day chosen for the wedding was highly significant:

> Monday for wealth,
> Tuesday for health,
> Wednesday the best day of all.
> Thursday for losses,
> Friday for crosses,
> Saturday no good at all.

Marriages took place during Lent or Advent only in very special circumstances, but this was more an ordinance of the Church than one of custom. A fine day presaged good fortune: 'Happy the bride the sun shines on.'

In the old days the guests travelled to the church in side-cars and a great concourse of horses and side-cars was referred to as 'a drag'. After the wedding, the bride and groom travelled in the first side-car. Sometimes they were 'roped'. A group of boys would hold a rope across the road and ask for a donation before allowing the bridal party to proceed on its way. The guests followed in a line of side-cars, and all returned to the bride's house where the celebrations continued into the early hours of the following day. Wren boys or straw boys often turned up at the wedding festivities, and these uninvited guests were treated to food and drink in return for the entertainment they provided. According to custom in many parts of Kerry, the bride did not return to her own home until one month had expired after the wedding day; then she visited her family and friends on what was traditionally called Month's Sunday. If a newly married couple did not go on a honeymoon (and very few did then) they usually absented themselves from mass on the first Sunday after the wedding.

When a girl acted as a bridesmaid in the thirties, it was thought important that she should marry during the subsequent twelve months, or she might end her days as a lonely old spinster. It was also a tradition that one tier of the wedding-cake had to be set aside for the first christening; if it was not preserved the marriage would be without issue.

Chalk Sunday was the first Sunday after Lent and was so called because 'all the old maids and bachelors who did not get married during Shrove were chalked on that Sunday. It was easy to identify them coming out of mass because they were chalked by the children, and the grown-ups too.' Newly married couples were expected to attend mass in their own church on that day.

Many ancient beliefs were associated with pregnancy. A pregnant woman should get a taste of every kind of food in the house; otherwise she would get an insatiable longing for the food that was denied her. If she saw a hare, the child would be born with a hare's lip, while if anything was thrown at her the offspring would be born with a pronounced birthmark. Pregnant beggar women were never sent away without being given an alm, and if a meal was in progress when they called they were allowed to sample everything on the table. When a pregnant woman gave alms to someone, the receiver would respond by saying, 'May the Lord bring you over the troubles of the year.' It was considered very inauspicious for a pregnant woman to enter a graveyard or carry dead meat home in her hands from the butcher.

The fairies were greatly feared at such times, since it was a well-known practice of theirs to steal a new-born baby and leave a changeling in its place. They were always on the look-out for good-looking babies who might one day become the wife of a fairy prince or the husband of a fairy princess, but in order to qualify for such high estate the babies had to be reared in fairyland. To counteract the influence of the fairies, the following procedures were sometimes adopted in the twenties and thirties: The wedding-ring of the expectant mother was removed and the clock was stopped. Every cupboard and box in the house was opened wide; if such boxes contained any money or small pieces of jewellery, they were zealously guarded by the father during the confinement and locked again when the first cries of the new-born child echoed through the house. It was usually considered advisable to watch over the infant from the moment of birth until the christening (which meant someone had to sit up all night) because it was during this brief period that the intervention of the fairies was most likely. The time lapse between birth and christening was very short because it was a tenet of faith that unbaptised babies went to Limbo, a fate no parent would wish upon their child; my mother told me that I was baptised two days after I was born, my head bathed with holy water from the large bowl upheld by a sculptured angel in St. John's Church in Tralee.

Even in the fifties, the women of the area still upheld the tradition of giving silver to a new-born baby, usually a florin or a half-crown at that time. Babies who laughed in their sleep were playing, my grandmother said, with the angels. It was unlucky to measure a new baby or to allow it to look in a mirror, and it was less than propitious to buy a new cradle for the first-born child of the family. Cots and cradles were relatively expensive items for poorer families so they must have been glad of this prohibition! The cot used in our family was brought over to us by an American uncle home on holidays. People who refused to act as a sponsor at a christening would never have a family of their own, but it was considered foolish to act as a sponsor twice in the same year. An older tradition required that when sponsors stood for a child at baptism, they were required to say 'I do renounce the devil' not 'I renounce him', because if the latter form was used 'the child might be taken by the joeys (fairies)'.

Children in the fifties were told nothing about pregnancy or childbirth. Instead we got colourful accounts of how we had come into the world. My sister, for instance, had been found beside the fishing-boat in a basket, wrapped in blankets, and my mother, being the kind-hearted woman she was, took pity on the poor abandoned creature and welcomed her into her heart and home. A head of cabbage in the vegetable patch was another favourite 'discovery' venue, while bold children had always been 'dragged in by the cat'. That was the sum total of our sex education.

The fifties brought the era of the dance ballroom. My sister and her friends were regular dance-goers, setting out on their bicycles in the late evening for dances in Castlemaine and Killorglin. A galaxy of glowing lights, moving like tiny stars along darkened country roads, was a familiar sight in the rural landscape of the time, and we children could hear the conversation and chatter of the cyclists echoing through the stillness of the evening. There might be talk about someone's new dress and how could she afford it? or scathing remarks about some fellow who was always late for a date, and of course the latest favourites from Elvis Presley and Chubby Chequers were discussed.

A friend of my sister's once had an unfortunate experience. She had just acquired a new dress, but when she set out for the dance she found her flash-light had failed completely. Undaunted, she began to cycle along the muddy roadway, but had not travelled very far when she crashed into an old man, one of the local characters, knocking him into the ditch. The new dress got a coating of mud but the old man, who usually wore a coarse bag on his head and looked vaguely like Archbishop Makarios of Cyprus (without the beard), had a field day telling and retelling the story. 'Hey, Paddy,' he would say to my father, 'She got me right in the ribs and the doctor says I won't be in the better of it for three years.' The number of years was variable, depending on mood and discretion. Luckily, as they say in Kerry, compensation had not yet set in, so we could all enjoy the joke.

11
Life in a Country Village

Under Cromwell's Act of Settlement, Colonel John Godfrey was required to 'settle' English Protestants on his lands. This he tried to do, not altogether successfully as we have seen. He also planned the development of a village, at the very gates of his Kilcoleman estate. A letter written in the year 1758 notes that: 'Mr Godfrey has lately built Milltown for tradesmen of all sorts and is endeavouring to establish some trade here for butter and fish for Cork.'

Though the butter trade did develop somewhat, Milltown, in common with so many other rural villages, remained in the grip of poverty for much of the nineteenth century, as Scots journalist, Henry Inglis, who visited the place in 1834, noted: 'Milltown is a very poor town, the property of Sir John Godfrey, who, from all that I could learn, has more the will then the power of benefiting it.'

By 1886 there were some six hundred and thirty-six people living in one hundred and eighteen houses, and the trades carried on included those of bootmaker, carpenter, cartwright, tinsmith, cooper, nailmaker and blacksmith. Successive generations of the same family carried on the same individual trade for decades, until their trade or service was rendered obsolete with the coming of the machine age. My aunt's husband, James O'Shea, was the blacksmith in the old chapel lane; he had inherited the craft from his father and grandfather, while a historical document relates that as far back as 1790 'James O'Shea, Smith, Old Chapel Lane' was making home-made ploughs.

In my youth, one of the most distinctive features of the small Irish town or village was the traditional shopfront. The designs were delightfully Victorian—entablatures resting on pilasters with decorative brackets, Doric or Ionic columns, round-headed mullions between vertical panes of glass with carved triangular panels above them. Fascia boards were made of timber, with painted, raised or sometimes carved lettering, often protected by a narrow length of glass.

There were some fine old shopfronts in both Milltown and Killorglin in the late fifties, and happily a few still survive. Particularly attractive are Falvey's Bar, Mangan's Drapery and O'Sullivan's Bar in Killorglin. Of the smaller Milltown shops one of the best remembered is that of H. Sugrue in Church Street. The wooden fascia board had the name of the owner painted on it in decorative lettering and, on either side, two artistic scrolls with the words 'Confectionery' and 'Groceries'. The shop itself aroused mixed feelings among the local school children. It sold bamboo canes to the school, enough to make it the bane of every schoolboy. On the other hand it was also the sweet shop, which helped to soften its image a little. Many of the shopfronts in Milltown were the work of the O'Donoghue brothers, who owned a workshop in the village. Their designs had a simple dignity, and the majority were in strong colour contrasts which caught the eye and did not fade; indeed it could be said that Kerry liked bright and brash colour schemes.

A nostalgic peep into the interior of one Milltown shop in the twenties is possible through the memories of Denis Sugrue:

> There was Clarke's Perfect Plug, Garryowen Twist, Wild Woodbines, Players and Gold Flake cigarettes, with glossy pictures inside the three-penny and six-penny packs. There was white cap snuff—snuff was a best-seller. Quaker oats and Van Houten cocoa competed with Lipton's Tea and Kavanagh's marmalade from Dundee, and the two-penny boxes of 'take me' matches. Pride of place on the shelves went to the attractive tins of NKM toffey, manufactured in the town of Listowel—these were the best-sellers in the sweet line, at twelve a penny. Every Tuesday the van arrived from Listowel with supplies for the small shops. The driver stayed overnight at the Godfrey Arms and was known affectionately as 'B and B'.

Larger towns such as Listowel had particularly fine

examples of decorative plasterwork on shops and hotels, much of it carried out by the McAuliffe brothers. They were responsible for the magnificent design on the Central Hotel, incorporating a traditional image of Ireland as a beautiful maiden, with a harp by her side and a wolfhound at her feet, a round tower with intricately executed windows and the words *Erin go Bragh* enclosed in a delightful tangle of fine Celtic interlace and shamrocks. Milltown's outstanding piece of plasterwork, that on the Crown Hotel, was lost to republican fervour in 1921. The Godfrey Arms Hotel, a halting station for Bianconi cars, and in later years the popular meeting-place of the East Lancashire Regiment, which was billeted in the local barracks in the early years of the century, also had a decorative sign with the name of the hotel and its insignia, but this too had vanished.

For much of the nineteenth century, Milltown had its distinctive market-house; there were four long-established fair days, on 26 April, 23 June, 23 August and 15 December.

Street fairs survived until the sixties but the establishment of a mart in 1959 for the buying and selling of livestock greatly diminished their significance. Other public buildings included the Bridewell and the Courthouse, both of which still survive. The Bridewell was described in a Victorian travel guide as 'a neat building, consisting of two day-rooms, two yards and six cells'. It was surrounded by an extensive perimeter wall. Petty Sessions were held in the Courthouse until the 1920s.

The most venerable of Milltown's churches is the ruined Abbey of Killagha, also known as the Abbey de Bello Loco, the abbey of the beautiful place. Built originally in 1215, its most famous features—the beautiful east window, the handsome double lancet window on the south side of the chancel and the square window of three lights on the western gable—were added in the early fifteenth century. The church is the only portion of the Abbey which still survives but people still come to admire the graceful sinuous lines of the east window with its ogee arch, splaying inwards, four mullions and lower lights. White Church, beside the Abbey, dates from 1734 but, according to Mrs. Ruth, was only in use for twenty-five years. The present Kilcoleman Church of Ireland chapel, with its elegant lofty square tower, surmounted by octangular pinnacles, was built in 1819. The Catholic church was renovated in 1893 at a cost of the then sizeable sum of £4000.

The Presentation Nuns came to Milltown in 1838. The building of the convent had begun in 1836, but when the five founder members arrived from Killarney two years later it was still unfinished. Their first school in Milltown was officially opened on 2 July 1838, when more than 300 children, led by parish priest Father Quill, recited the litany of Our Lady. The first superioress was Mother Teresa Kelly.

Just four months later, a violent storm swept in from the Atlantic and demolished the greater part of the newly erected convent, as well as doing extensive damage to other buildings in the village. Further storms during the month of January 1839 did not help matters, but with the aid of parish contributions and the support of 'many wealthy lay persons', the convent was eventually rebuilt, this time on a larger scale than originally intended. The number of children on the roll book for the year 1874 was 430, while the average attendance figures ranged from 200 to 250.

The thatched cottage continued to be a feature of rural Ireland until well into the forties. Thatching was an activity that needed calm settled weather, giving rise to the old proverb *Ní hí lá na gaoithe, lá na scoilbe*, the day of the wind is not the day for thatching. The thatcher roofed with reeds or wheaten straw, put up in courses and held together with spars, and his craft was highly regarded. My uncle, who was an expert thatcher, used reeds, which were in plentiful supply near the riverside. My grandfather, John D., had also been a thatcher. 'He used to thatch houses all over Callinafercy and up in Dromin and everywhere, and, *mo léir*, he had no bicycle but had to walk long distances.'

The lifespan of a newly thatched roof depended largely on location. Houses close to the wind-battered coastline needed regular attention, while others further inland required far less. One of our neighbours—whose cottage was on the edge of the Laune—always seemed to be repairing his thatched roof.

There were many thatched houses in our locality. One of the most beautiful was a tiny white-washed cottage, with windows outlined in pastel pink. Set in a garden which was a patchwork of colour and enclosed by a hedge which had been expertly shaped into a row of brooding hens, complete with enamel eyes, it might have come straight from the pages of Hans Anderson or Grimm. It became famous both nationally and internationally and was used as a backdrop for the Cardiff Male Boys' Choir when they were filmed on location in the area. The twenty-five members stood on the narrow road outside the cottage and sang traditional songs and ballads such as *I Hear You Calling Me* (the old John McCormack favourite) and *The Wild Rover*.

'A cooper without a compass is like a banker without a pen' was a saying associated with the craft of the cooper. The Milltown area supplied the Cork butter market for many years, hence the necessity for churns and barrels, the latter being used to transport the butter. Churns were made from staves bound with hoops and various designs were popular in different parts of the country. The cooper also made piggins and noggins—small drinking-vessels in which one stave was left longer than the others and served as a convenient handle.

The forge was very much a meeting-place for the men of the district. Here the blacksmith made the bands or hoops for the cooper's barrels, as well as a great variety of implements for various trades, including pitchforks, scythes, and griddles for making bread. Indeed, a country blacksmith could turn his hand to practically anything. When the handle of our cast-iron kettle broke, my father took it to Uncle James for repair. An old lady who lived nearby had an exquisitely patterned red and blue dish which he had expertly sewn together with stitches of iron wire.

The blacksmith's main job was shoeing. There was always a horse in the forge in Milltown in the late fifties and early sixties, and Uncle James had a great rapport with these strong muscular work horses. I loved animals, but horses and donkeys were a consuming passion with my cousin James, and like his father he had a way with them. He was always patting and stroking and talking to them, while his father's face dripped with sweat as he forged a shoe in the red-hot fire. He knew all the horses in the village, not only by name but also by temperament and character. There was a closeness there, a bond between boy and animal that was immediately apparent. Our little brown donkey was regularly shod in the forge and my father saw to it too that his hooves were kept trimmed and cut; he hated to see donkeys with long hooves, as he knew that this made them suffer unnecessary pain. The grey donkey which succeeded our brown donkey was a great favourite with James, and when she gave birth to a rare and beautiful snow-white foal, he was even more delighted than we were.

Milltown was for long the centre of a thriving linen industry. When the flax was harvested it was soaked in a wet boggy place and then spread out in a field or along a hedgerow as part of the bleaching process—there are still place-names such as Bleach Road and Bleach Lane in the locality. Indeed the former gained a certain notoriety in the twenties and thirties for being the favourite haunt of courting couples; one parish priest was known to declare: 'Wherever the devil is by day, he's in Bleach Road by night.' When the flax was finally prepared, it was spun into petticoats and dresses, having been dyed with the leaves of the alder-tree or some other herb.

Older crafts such as those of the nailmaker and the saddler died away in Milltown in the sixties. Stephen Potter, the local saddler, was widely known for his singing while he worked, while nails made by the Raymond Brothers reappear now and then, bringing back many memories for the older people, who remember the family with affection. The wood-turner made small wooden vessels, mainly from beech, which was the favourite wood. Dan Donoghue was the wood-carver of Milltown; he made the local shopfronts and the altar and pews in the convent oratory. Baskets for carrying potatoes, fruit, eggs and groceries were made from willows which had been carefully dried. Candles were made in iron moulds; a cord was passed down through the melted fat and then allowed to harden. Shoemakers made and mended shoes, using the shoemaker's last; 'ould Ted Kennedy', who lived in a long low thatched cottage in the twenties, was one of the last in the Callinafercy area. Tailors flourished on a true made-to-measure basis and in the fifties my father's suits were still made by a tailor in Killorglin.

In my youth many old men could produce an expertly finished *sugán* chair with its seat of interwoven straw, and indeed most of the cottage and farmhouse furniture was handcrafted by local carpenters during the first half of the present century. Dressers, tables and chairs, as well as the ubiquitous three-legged stool were all made. The travelling people were skilled in a wide range of crafts, particularly that of the tinsmith. They not only offered a variety of household utensils such as 'gallons' (a container that held a gallon), buckets and quart measures for sale but they were also willing to undertake repair work on leaking kettles, pans and saucepans. Sweets such as cloves and bull's eyes came in big silvery tins and were referred to as 'gallon sweets'; my mother often asked one of the local shops to keep her a gallon when all its contents had been sold. Another time I might be sent to purchase a 'penny tinker', a circular piece of metal that was used to plug a leak in a gallon or a tin bath.

The clocksmith was more than happy when he was allowed to operate on a clock that had not ticked for years. The back of the clock was removed and the various mechanisms and springs carefully laid out in sequence on a sheet of newspaper on the table, before they were reassembled with surgical precision.

Many of the old ladies of the district were expert lace and crochet-makers. The convent of the Poor Clares at Kenmare was perhaps the first lace-making centre in Kerry, and an industrial school was established there in 1864. Mother O'Hagan was the guiding force behind Kenmare needle-point, which gradually became known as *Point d'Irlandaise* and was celebrated worldwide for its delicacy of design and execution. Our neighbour Mary was always doing crochet, usually centre-pieces for tables or dressing-tables, while my mother made pictures using different coloured cloths. I remember one vividly—a bright blue sky with seagulls flying by; a little thatched cottage and a boat on the tide; fields, brown and green; and two happy children on their way home from school.

In the old days (pre-1950 or so), the Lenten mission was one of the most important events on the Church calendar. A neighbour told me about the one in Milltown:

> People used rise early to go to the morning mass; they'd go to two masses, wan in the morning and wan in the evening. The first sermon was nearly always about Hell and Damnation. There would always be wan good preacher and wan not so good. The missioners were nice to talk to, but they frightened the life out of the people with their sermons. They were dead against 'company keeping', as they called it. The people gave up dancing and cards the week of the mission. And they'd be runnin' for the box (confession box), and there would be that much of a crowd you'd have a struggle to get near the stalls.'

There are other interesting memories of that mission.

> They'd visit the old people and the parish priest drove um around in his horse and trap. People bought holy pictures and statues and scapulars at the mission—they'd be enrolled in the scapulars during the mission, and they'd hold up their purchases to have um blessed during wan of the masses. The missioners spent a week in Milltown and a week in Listry, and the people paid extra at the door of the church to keep um for that time.

> There was this story told about a missioner, and I suppose 'twas only a story. He stood up in the pulpit and says he, very seriously, 'I'd like to remind everywan present that all the people in this parish will die wan day.' There was this fella sittin' almost directly undernate him and he started to laugh. Well, the priest got very

cross and he asked him why was he laughing at such a serious statement. 'Sure, I'm not from this parish at all, Father,' says he.

Bob Knightly said that the missioners didn't object to dances if they 'were held in a nice manner', but the parish priest, Father Carmody, went around and raided the houses. It was said on one such occasion that the man of the house quenched the lamp when the priest came in and there was never any luck in the place afterwards; not one of the children was reared in that house.

There were humorous stories about Father Carmody, too:

Wan New Year's morning there was a couple of people at the gates of the church, waiting for Father Carmody. A man from Listry came down in his donkey and cart— the poor man was after gettin' a few shillings some place and he was almost fallin' out of the cart with the drink that was on him. 'Woe betide you, Mick B—!' says Father Carmody. 'The same to you, Father,' says poor Mick, thinkin' he was after gettin' a great blessin' and wantin' to return the compliment.

Then there was the story of the money that had been found by an honest parishioner, who immediately reported the matter to his parish priest!

' 'Tisn't a large sum, by no manes,' says Father Carmody, 'but tell me did you advertise it at all?'

'No, Father,' says the lad, 'but I told three women and sure that's the same thing.'

It was probably only a story, but story or not it would hardly be permissible today.

The GAA is part of the Kerry tradition. Both Milltown and Castlemaine competed as separate clubs in the County Championship of 1890, and it was fifty-seven years before the two clubs amalgamated to form Milltown-Castlemaine. When Kerry played Roscommon in the All-Ireland Final

of 1946, there were two locals on the Kerry team, Brendan
Kelliher and Paddy Burke, the latter scoring one of the two
vital goals which earned Kerry a replay, and which they
duly won. Paddy Burke became a local hero, and a local
poet burst into song:

> The full forward from Milltown
>   Strode on to the field,
> Green and gold were his colours,
>   To no back would he yield,
> To play for the Kingdom
>   And bring home the crown.
> So three cheers for our forward—
> Young Burke from Milltown.

In 1961, the Milltown-Castlemaine GAA Club purchased
its own playing field; Father McCluskey, who was the curate
in Milltown at the time, was very much the driving force
behind that far-sighted venture.

Junior football was greatly encouraged by the Presentation
Brothers, who had been in Milltown since the mid-
nineteenth century, when the Presentation Monastery was
built. A team drawn from Callinafercy National School and
the Monastery National School won the first mid-Kerry
Schools League in 1954. Amongst the brothers involved
with local football teams were Brothers Justin, Fergal and
Angus.

No account of life in a country village would be complete
without mentioning that most Irish or all Irish institutions—
the pub. There were seven public houses in Milltown, while
Killorglin had a staggering twenty-four. It was unlikely, to
say the least of it, that anyone would die of the thirst! Larkins
was the favourite pub for GAA enthusiasts, while Langfords
had an old-world ambiance, with a decorative pendulum
clock, polished woodwork, mirrors and pictures. Many
public houses had little secluded corners, called snugs, where
a small group could enjoy their drinks in relative privacy.

In the days when women, officially at any rate, did not drink, snugs were the perfect solution, offering indulgence with anonymity; naturally, a woman had to be over a certain age, even for snug drinking, if one was not to encounter the raised eyebrow.

If I paint a too idyllic picture of life in a small Irish village, perhaps it is because time has coloured the memories of those days a rosy-tinted hue, and the imperfections have faded like one of the old photographs that we used to treasure. There must have been times when churns leaked, shoes pinched, jackets were too tight in the arms, and the clockmaker didn't manage to put all the bits and pieces together again. But, on balance, it still seems to me that those *were* good days. A spirit of harmony and helpfulness prevailed. Though one's economic status inevitably determined one's social class, character and ability were also valued; if one had no ability, there was an understanding acceptance that not everyone is perfect and that there must be room at the inn for all.

The people I grew up among rejoiced in individuality, even eccentricity, because of the colour it gave to our lives; but the other side of the coin was an intolerance that I only later came to comprehend.

The penny catechism had disappeared when I was a child, but even in the late fifties and early sixties we were left in no doubt that Catholicism was the one and only road to salvation and that those of other faiths, the poor unfortunates, were automatically condemned to some form of eternal damnation. I know that even as a child it struck me as curious that people who differed so little from ourselves were doomed for professing beliefs which, though not Catholic, were Christian.

The Church was also more class-conscious than we were. Though our society didn't quite rise to the rich man in his castle, the strong farmer on his fruitful acres was more

I Heard the Wild Birds Sing

acceptable than the poor man, still milling around the gates. A curious practice of those days was the reading out, at a certain Sunday mass each year, the list of those who had given parish dues. The priest went through the names, townland by townland, mentioning the amount of the contribution after each name. No comment was ever made about the generosity (or lack of it) of a particular donation. After mass the list was, of course, much discussed, though happily the principal focus was on those of substantial means who were adjudged to have been niggardly in their contributions. The offerings of the less well-off were given the respect of silence.

Even death, that great leveller, could not cross the dividing lines. When Catholics attended the funeral of a Protestant neighbour they were forbidden to enter the Protestant church or the graveyard; to do so was considered sinful. This was the norm, even in Milltown where relations between Catholic and Protestant were very cordial. However, when the remains of a Catholic neighbour were removed to our church, Mrs. Ruth, who was a Protestant, often made a point of joining in the prayers with us.

Charity, though preached, was not practiced in certain instances, usually those with a sexual dimension. As children, we knew nothing of these facts of life; it was only in later years that we heard how young unmarried girls who had become pregnant had been regarded as having brought disgrace on their families. The principal concern of the girl's parents on such occasions was usually to see that she was married as swiftly and as furtively as possible. There was a story of a young pregnant girl in the Milltown area who had, on the insistence of her parents, been obliged to set out under a veil of secrecy on a winter's dawn to be married to the father of her child. This was the darker side of Irish life, though a commitment to respectability ensured it did not emerge to trouble us.

All this, let me hasten to add, represented Church

thinking—at the top. The priests and nuns with whom we had dealings were, in the main, kindly and helpful, usually with a greater understanding of the trials and tribulations of the life practical as opposed to the life theoretical.

When I look back over the changes that the years have brought, perhaps nothing is quite as dramatic as the change in the position of women. My mother's generation was happy and fulfilled as homemakers (which was just as well as there was usually no alternative!) but there must have been some who felt restricted and powerless and who longed for careers and opportunities outside the home. Fifty years or so ago, the thought of a man on the moon and a woman President would have been undreamt of in their philosophies.

Perhaps, as it is time to go, we should salute *Mná na hEireann* and their inexorable march towards a better world. I know it will be a more honest world. I hope it will be as happy as the one that my parents and all the people of my childhood created for me.

I will always be grateful that I heard the wild birds sing.

Envoi

My mother died in the springtime, in March, eighteen years to the month after my father's death. She was waked at home and, once again, the fragrance of the flowering currant mingled with the scent of the tallow from the lighted candles, creating an exotic kind of incense. Seven candles shone at her bedside, some of them, following the time-honoured tradition, borrowed from neighbours. I made a wreath with flowers from her much-loved garden, to place beside the simple arrangement of daffodils and grape hyacinths from Mrs. Ruth's garden.

If I am sorry that she did not live to see the publication of this book, at least I have the consolation that she shared in this evocation of times past. It is, in a way, her book as much as mine; through it, she and my father will always be alive, just as I remember them.

Sometimes I see you in that fabulous field,
The elders laden with clusters of white.
'We'll make it into grasscocks soon,' you say,
Turning the hay with the pike.

Or I see us together in the shadow of the fort,
Bewitched by the pink-blossomed crab.
The small black cows come and wonder for a moment,
And the fairy wind sighs through the grass.

Sometimes in the stillness of evening,
When the sun paints a rose on the tide,
I watch you bathe your feet in the water,
Sensing things eternal in the plaintive curlew's cry.

Or I see you in the little cottage garden—
Oh! a magical place so serene.
An orange-billed blackbird whistles from the sycamore,
You listen, and smile like a child in a dream.

Often I hear you calling to the turkeys,
And the hens come running too.
'That brown hen lays a grand egg,' you say,
Eggs, like treasures from a Pharoah's tomb.

I see how the silver scales of the salmon,
Mean more to you than pockets of gold.
For these are the sons of the Salmon of Knowledge,
That gladdened the heart of Fionn in the glorious days
    of old.

And sometimes I see you coming from the well,
Bluebells, like stars, in your hand.
Sky-blue symbols for the mother of love,
The One who will always understand.

You are not dead but live in memory and love,
Your days shall be glad evermore.
Heavenly days of flowers and country songs,
And walking in waves that wash the eternal shore.

PATRICK O'SULLIVAN was born and brought up in Callinafercy, where he still lives. He has an Honours Degree in history and Latin, from University College, Cork, and qualified as a secondary school teacher. He has taught part time in a number of schools.

A prizewinner at Listowel Writers' Week in 1988, *I Heard the Wild Birds Sing,* is his third book; his two previous books—*The Golden Horse of the Gods* and *The Adventures of Haggerty*—both published by Glendale, were for children. He has also published articles in newspapers and magazines in Ireland and the UK.

He is not the first writer in his family; his uncle and grand-uncle both wrote poetry and songs in Irish and English.

He is keenly interested in the environment, in the birds, animals and flowers of his native countryside, and *I Heard the Wild Birds Sing* will appeal equally to lovers of wild life and those interested in the colourful folk culture of an older generation.

AL O'DONNELL is Senior Graphics Designer at Radio Telefis Eireann. He has illustrated a number of books including *The Adventures of Henry & Sam & Mr. Fielding* and *Barney the Hedgehog*, which were published by The Children's Press.

His spare time love is music and he composes, writes lyrics and performs solo.